THE SOUTHERN WAY

CONTENTS

© Kevin Robertson (Noodle Books) and the various contributors 2010

ISBN 978-1-906419-42-4

First published in 2010 by Kevin Robertson

under the **NOODLE BOOKS** imprint

PO Box 279

Corhampton

SOUTHAMPTON

SO32 3Z

www.noodlebooks.co.uk

editorial@thesouthernway.co.uk

Printed in England by

Ian Allan Printing Ltd

Hersham, Surrey

Every so often something comes along image-wise that is both stunning and unexpected. This would certainly fit the criteria, 'D15' 4-4-0 No 30465 at the Ocean Terminal Southampton. The view is undated, although a bit of basic detective work means it can only be between 1950 and 1956. More of like quality from the same source very soon.   Henry Meyer

Front Cover - *Proudly displaying a red '83D' Plymouth Laira and Launceston shedplate, 'N'. No 31835 waits - for repair / assessment or condemnation perhaps, at the front of Eastleigh Works.*   Tim Stubbs

Rear Cover - *"What a difference ……...(a few decades)... make..." What might well have been thought the end for No. 34067 'Tangmere' on the scrap road at Eastleigh in 1964. One of ten member so the class withdrawn in 1963 and seen here with its nameplate removed and associated shield crudely cut out. The centre pair of tender wheels have been extracted no doubt for use on another member of the class, possibly any other number components were likewise taken off. The identity of the sister engine on the left is not confirmed, although it may well have been 34068 withdrawn around the same time. No 34067 eventually found its way to Woodham Bros. at Barry, from where it was rescued for preservation.*

Keeping with our 'arty' theme still, this the work of the professional. Simply entitled 'Waterloo Station, 1934'. The work of Emil Otto Hoppé. (For those with access to the internet, it is well worth putting the name Emil Otto Hoppé, or an abbreviation thereof, into a search engine. Born in Germany in 1872, his work covers several continents with a style nowadays recognised as one of the true greats in portraying photography as an art form.)

Editorial Introduction

It is always a pleasure to open the post, I should say e-mails of course as well, to be greeted by something unexpected and pleasing. Sometimes these things arrive totally unexpected, other times anticipated, especially when one had perhaps almost given up hope of a response or successful conclusion.

Certainly within the first category are the opening views of Peckham Rye, a chance e-mail and the results you will see within these pages. Coincidentally, whilst this issue was being put together, there was thread on the Southern e-mail group concerning restoration of the station as part of a general redevelopment of the site. The work has been inspired and led by Benedict O'Looney, a local architect and historian, also a member of the Peckham Society. It will be interesting to watch developments.

Harking back to my opening paragraph, and now to matters which we had perhaps ever given up of seeing. In this category I would place the photographs that appear in this issue as 'Winchester Part 2.' Years ago I recall seeing a set of these images but had almost forgotten when and where. A chance conversation and the results appear from Page 70 onwards.

On a similar tact, regular readers will recall the question I raised over the use of wheel-tappers on the Southern. Here we were delighted to receive a call from another friend, George Voller of Fareham. George is a long time volunteer and supporter of the Talyllyn Railway, but evidently also has some softness for the Southern! He comments, "I am almost certain I recall hearing a wheel tapper at work at Salisbury when travelling to the West on holiday. But I know I heard one at Exeter in the time when the service was stationary and the train was in the process of being divided. Whilst waiting at Exeter we would also be visited by a Golden Retriever who would calmly wander through the train collecting on behalf of Woking Homes. The dog was of a very placid nature and certainly not spooked by the normal station sounds or ringing clang from underneath." We later heard from another friend, Brian Drysdall, that wheel-tappers were definitely present at Salisbury, "When we were train spotting we got used to the sound of the hammer associated with a normal and occasional defective wheel."

Then from Richard Foot, "I refer to your lead article in the latest issue of The Southern Way (No. 11) and can vouch to the fact that wheeltappers operated at Waterloo Station. I can clearly remember, in the late 1950s / early 1960s, a man with a hammer on a long handle striking all the wheels on the off side of the carriages standing at the platform. I assume he did this over the electrified third rail which I suspect was boarded on both sides. How he managed to check the wheels nearest the platform remains a mystery. Perhaps they didn't bother. I hope this helps to throw some light on the question." Finally from Vic Freemantle, "When still in short trousers in the mid to late 1950s on days out to the Seaside from Eastleigh with Family Weekly Runabout tickets, (stiff green cards), I still have a vivid picture in my mind of seeing such a Wheel-tapper at Bournemouth Central. Cloth cap, jacket over bib & tucker work wear, with a smooth /calculated swing of a clean looking longish wood handled shiny hammer. Not looking too tall up against the side of the coaches as he walked steadily along the six foot of the train in the opposite platform, striking every wheel and often checking underneath. As your readers will know, this would be the ideal station for such checks as he would be able to do one side of the Down train at Central before it split for West and Weymouth. He would then be able to check the other side of the train on its return and coupling ready for the Up working back to Waterloo. The SR even in BR times still keeping most coach stock in sets no doubt, some form of record may well have been made/kept. You may of course get a more professional response but hope this of interest, the Bournemouth man may have been the last of his kind, I never ever remember seeing one at Eastleigh. Perhaps due to the presence of the through lines there being used more frequently by fast trains and of course Eastleigh had actual Carriage Sidings away from public eyes and ears."

As ever, thank you all for your contributions, large or small. I am delighted to report material continues to arrive, but with each issue a fair amount is of course used. However, in the past few weeks it has been a pleasure to renew several acquaintances which I am hopeful will bear fruit in the future.

You will note, that as with Issue No. 11, we have gone over our standard 100 sides again this month. I don't expect anyone will mind too much. The rationale was again to try a bit of a catch-up, we have not quite succeeded but I hope what you see will make the effort of the extra page turning involved worthwhile. Should you wish to comment, praise or berate the Editor on any topic whatsoever, then we also have a new contact point which will be operational by the time you read this.

editorial@thesouthernway.co.uk

The same details appear on Page 1. Previous contact points, as well as letter and telephone continue to be welcome.

Normally of course we leave comments and the like to our 'Rebuilt' pages, but a few matters arising from issue 11 are such that they warrant a place here instead. Firstly to Martin Breakspear, I sincerely apologise for the misspelling of your name in the excellent 'Pull-Push' article. This piece has generated much favourable comment and feedback, so much so that a follow up with material from Gerry Bixlex amongst others, is scheduled for Issue 14. I trust several of you will also have spotted the deliberate mistake in Martin's article. We did it, not him, left and rights on the various air-pipes on page 33. Apart from Martin, two of us saw it and two of us missed it. Again apologies. Now some extra bits from John Davenport of Woking, "..the signalman seen handing the staff to the driver on page 24 of Issue 11 was relief man Ernie Standford - No. 32379 was on the other end of the train." I never cease to be amazed at the breath of knowledge of all. Thank you.

As this is the final issue of 2010, it may be a little early to wish everyone the compliments of the season, but what I can safely say is there will be plenty to look forward to in 2011. Mishaps - on the railway that is, we have a-plenty, as well as hoped for pieces on locomotive availability, more reminiscences and several excellent photo features. Someone in the past had a phrase, "We're getting there", I hope we in turn might have nearly arrived.

Kevin Robertson

PECKHAM RYE
Circa 1870

This and the following double page: two wonderful 19th century views of Peckham Rye circa 1870.

The first railway here had been the LCDR route from Herne Hill to Elephant and Castle in 1862. The station at Peckham Rye opened in 1865 - possibly in August. The following year, the LBSCR opened their own station alongside, by which time also this palatial station building, described as 'Victorian Romanesque' in style, had appeared between the two lines. Whether it was a joint structure is uncertain. At this stage the main building appears to be a mirror image of itself front to back, although in later years various alterations and additions, chimneys for example were added. The view on this page was taken from Rye Lane which passes under both companies' lines and was the only public access to the station. To the left are the LBSCR platforms on the route from Tulse Hill to London Bridge, the LCDR platforms on the right.

Overleaf: Believed to be No. 71, a Sharps 2-4-0 of 1848. The engine is seen at the head of what may be a London Bridge train. This particular engine survived until 1871 and so may therefore be of assistance in dating the views - assuming of course both were taken at the same time.

The images were kindly loaned by Andrew Wells who had acquired them some 40 odd years ago from an elderly lady, Mrs Hammond. Andrew advises Mr Hammond used to run a paperstall at the station, although nothing else is known of their history.

After their use here in *SOUTHERN WAY* the views will be deposited in the Bluebell Railway Archive.

SOUTHERN RAILWAY

THREE DIMENSIONAL PUBLICITY

TONY HILLMAN

What comes to mind when the words "Southern Railway publicity" are mentioned? Is it a copy of "Hints for Holidays", a colourful leaflet describing the numerous reasons for visiting some coastal resort or a humble handbill? The Southern Railway produced many thousands of different paper based advertising items, but also produced a range of advertising material of a three-dimensional nature. This article describes non-paper based Southern Railway advertising.

Jigsaws

Unlike the Great Western Railway, who produced numerous wooden jigsaws, the Southern Railway only produced two jigsaws which can be considered as official. Both used the same picture showing the Golden Arrow hauled by the Lord Nelson class locomotive Sir Richard Grenville.

First advertised by the Southern Railway in December 1929, the 24" by 9" jigsaw was produced by Photochrome with 160 wooden pieces. Priced at 5/-, the jigsaw was available from the Advertising Department, Waterloo. A poster was produced to advertise the Golden Arrow which includes reference to the jigsaw. (This poster has been produced as a modern postcard by Mayfair Cards of London, reference BB144).

Chad Valley produced a smaller pocket-sized version with 40 wooden pieces for sale to passengers on the Golden Arrow and cross Channel ferries.

Victory produced a jigsaw of the Atlantic Coast Express, showing a scene at Seaton Junction. Even though it used the same image as a photograph which appeared in the February 1937 edition of the 'Southern Railway Magazine', it is probably not an official item as no evidence can be found of the Southern Railway advertising or selling it. (See also page 17.)

The text describes the photograph as: "On the left S15 No. 824. Main Line - King Arthur No. 451. In the platform is a Templecombe to Exeter stopper and on the right a Stroudley D1 0-4-2 tank.

A leaflet was also included which gave some details of the timings and locomotives that hauled the Atlantic Coast Express.

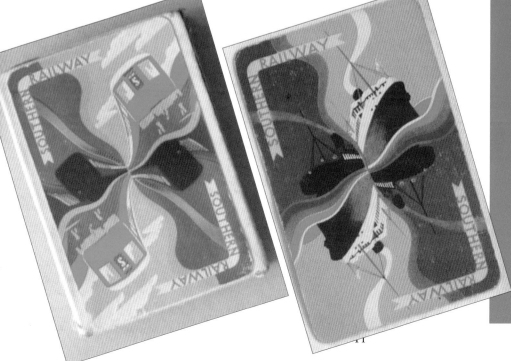

Playing Cards

Waddingtons produced two sets of playing cards for the Southern Railway. Both have similar designs, one advertising Southern Electric and the other Southern Ships.

With no advertisements known for these cards it is difficult to date them. The box bears slogans such as "Why not build your home in the electrified area?" The Southern Railway also used similar advertising during the early 1930s.

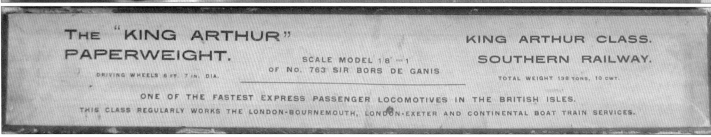

THE "KING ARTHUR" PAPERWEIGHT.

DRIVING WHEELS 6 FT. 7 IN. DIA.

SCALE MODEL 1/8″—1
OF No. 763 SIR BORS DE GANIS

KING ARTHUR CLASS.
SOUTHERN RAILWAY.

TOTAL WEIGHT 138 TONS. 10 CWT.

ONE OF THE FASTEST EXPRESS PASSENGER LOCOMOTIVES IN THE BRITISH ISLES.
THIS CLASS REGULARLY WORKS THE LONDON-BOURNEMOUTH, LONDON-EXETER AND CONTINENTAL BOAT TRAIN SERVICES.

The King Arthur Paperweight.
This was produced early in 1926 and advertised as, "The neatest and most useful adjunct to your desk equipment". The paperweight was claimed to be an exact scale model of No. 763, 'Sir Bors de Ganis.'
At this time the Southern Railway often advertised in the 'Railway Magazine' and the model was noted as available to the public for 5/-. This figure was reduced to 2/6d in a June 1929 advertisement, when, it was claimed, there was only 100 left to sell. (Two copies of the model were given as consolation prizes to the two members of staff who were the runners up in the 1925 SR competition to name the new train that would become the 'ACE'. The winner, Guard Rowland from Waterloo, received £3 3s.)

Model Ships. The waterline models of the Southern Railway Steamers, 'Canterbury', 'Isle of Jersey' and 'Isle of Guernsey' were produced by Messrs. Bassett-Lowke to a scale of 75ft to 1in. They were boxed and sold for 5/-. No official mention or advertisements can be found for these models. The box carried the words 'Southern Railway' in its traditional sunshine lettering, which could mean that the production of these models had some official backing. A very brief description of the vessel was contained on the label.

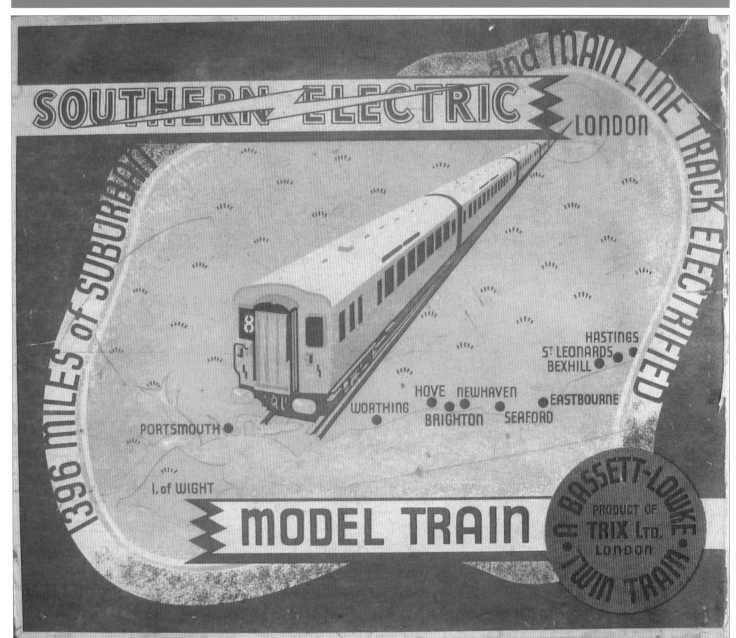

Model Electric Train The February 1937 edition of the 'Southern Railway Magazine' included an article on the Bassett-Lowke produced Trix Twin OO gauge Southern Electric Model Train Set: "Mr C Grasemann, Advertising Officer of the Southern Railway, was quick to realise the potentialities of this novelty, and, in collaboration with him, Messrs. Bassett-Lowke, Ltd., have just placed on the market an actual scale model, representing one of the new electric trains, which will run on the London - Portsmouth service. The set is made up in an attractive box covered with green enamelled paper and a multicoloured label specially designed by the Southern Railway Company."

The set cost 55/- and included a complimentary copy of the 8 page Southern Railway publication *The Evolution of the World's Largest Suburban Electrified Railway.* A set was put on show at Waterloo Station. The green enamelled paper used for the box was made from Celilynd that wears badly. This means that most of the boxes that survive are in a poor condition.

Ashtrays - There are five known advertising ashtrays. Two (Nos. 1 & 2) are made from *Omnite Ware,* a material very like bakelite. Note that the wording on the first ashtray is concave while on the second it is convex. These were, presumably, used in areas where the public would congregate: station restaurants etc. The 'South for Sunshine' wording is a classic Southern Railway advertising slogan.

The brass Southern Railway ashtray (3), was probably used similarly to Nos. 1 and 2, and may have predated them. The silver ashtray (4) was produced for the Southampton Docks Centenary in 1938. It was, almost certainly, sold or given away to visitors to the Centenary celebrations.

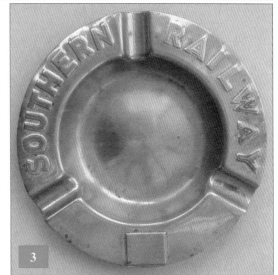

Not available to the public, but included here for completeness is the ashtray numbered (5). The Southern Sales League was a scheme whereby station staff competed against other stations to increase revenue. This ashtray was given the stations doing best in the competition. It was only produced in 1938.

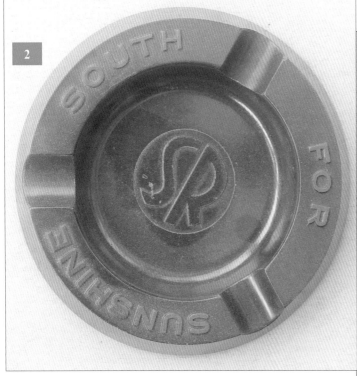

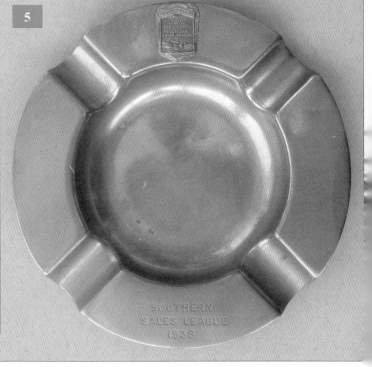

The black and white photograph that formed the basis for the jigsaw referred to on pages 10/11. (The most obvious alteration between the original and coloured reproduction being the smoke effect from the locomotives.) The location has been incorrectly stated elsewhere as being Wimbledon, but it is clearly Seaton Junction. As referred to earlier, what was probably its first published use was in the February 1937 'Southern Railway Magazine' (Vol. XV No. 170) to accompany a four page article by Frank E. Box entitled, 'The 10.35 am Waterloo to Ilfracombe'.

Interestingly, whilst the caption referred to the main subject being the 'Atlantic Coast Express', the title of the article did not. A footnote though added, "The 10.35 am from Waterloo runs in the summer service and from Monday to Friday carries the North Devon and North Cornwall portions of the 'Atlantic Coast Express'. On Saturdays the train is further sub-divided, the 10.35 am running to Ilfracombe, the 10.45 am to Padstow, and the 11.00 am to Plymouth, Bude and Torrington. In the winter service, the 'Atlantic Coast express' leaves at 11.00 am for all parts." (See also, item No. 5427 on page 32.)

The booklet cover, left, comes from the 1937 Southern Railway publication, "An illustrated account of what is seen from the window of the Atlantic Coast Express". By S P B Mais, with illustrations - by Anna Zinkeisen. Courtesy Peter Bailey.

17

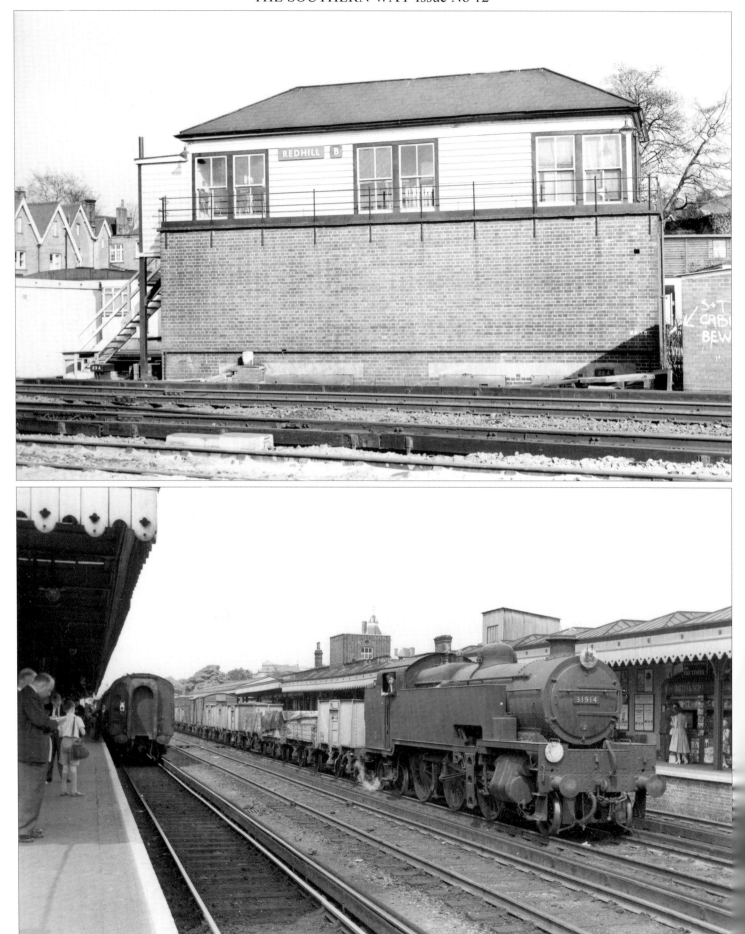

FROM REDHILL 'B' to THREE BRIDGES - via DORKING TOWN, MERSTHAM AND REDHILL 'A'

Michael Harvey

August 1958 saw the start of my career in signalling, beginning in the time-honoured way as a Booking Boy at one of the busy main line boxes: in my case this was Redhill 'B', a former South Eastern structure located in the 'V' of the junction between the Reigate and main lines at the south end of Redhill station. The box might have been original although the frame certainly was not, as consequent to layout changes and electrification in 1932, the smaller South Eastern lever frame had been replaced by a rearward facing 85 lever 'Westinghouse' installation. (The name Redhill 'B' had been carried since 25 November 1956: prior to this the two Redhill boxes had been referred to as No 1 and No 2.)

The box at Redhill 'B' controlled the junctions between the main lines, the Reigate and Tonbridge branches and the divergence of the through and platform lines. Additional to this were the connections to the up yard, the loco shed exit, several sidings, plus ground frame releases for the down yard and carriage sidings. Understandably, then, to a newcomer, 'B' box was a noisy and confusing place, block working was in force on all running lines, and the cacophony of ringing bells, crashing levers and frequent phone calls was almost overwhelming.

Inside, the desk for the booking boy was about midway along the box, sitting with his back to the main line and facing the large illuminated diagram on which all the running lines were shown as track-circuited. Apart from the signal box register, there was also a telephone concentrator on the desk for the several phone lines which came into the box.

The signals were semaphore throughout, the two farthest away being motor-operated. We also had one set of points that was motor worked: all the others operated by rodding from the frame, or mechanically worked, as the signalmen described it.

Block working on the main lines through Redhill was maintained by the well-known Sykes 'Lock & Block' instruments and quite noisy in operation. On these, 'line clear' or 'blocked' labels dropped into the display aperture, and were connected to the levers by rods. For the branch lines, standard Southern Region three-position block was used to Reigate, while an antique Walker's instrument complete with miniature signal to show 'line clear' was used on the Tonbridge route.

Because of the both the density and complexity of the service, some form of train describer was essential for the main line: this was provided by another Walker's instrument having a clock face with 12 different descriptions available. Thus descriptions were sent to and received from Earlswood, the next box south, and Redhill 'A' at the London end of the station. Train descriptions were sent when a train was offered-on to the box in advance, in addition descriptions were received from Coulsdon North box, thus giving advanced warning of down trains.

As booking boy, my job entailed recording all the bell codes sent or received by us. The times were entered onto the train register sheets, with separate sheets for the up and down lines. I also dealt with most of the phone calls: for example asking permission from the shunter for a freight to enter the up yard. It was the practice for us to ask the loco shed foreman when we needed the engines for trains departing from Redhill. This meant a good knowledge of the actual engine workings, as some locomotives did not go to shed after arrival and instead went straight on to their next service. We also had to phone over to the control office with the arrival and departure times of the branch trains.

The complex workings at Redhill meant that a wide variety of different bell codes had to be recorded. For example, when a Tonbridge to Reading train arrived and the engine had been released, 'A' box would send '2-1-3' "Engine arrived" to 'B' box, while when it had left, 'B' box sent '3-2-3' "Train drawn back clear of section" to 'A' box. There were also a number of local codes in use to cover every conceivable right and wrong direction shunt move.

Despite having the main lines electrified, a surprise for me was the high level of steam working. Indeed it seemed there was always a loco present in the station or up yard. Perhaps not surprising really, as during the morning rush, from about 07.00 to 09.40, there were 12 steam arrivals, 7 departures, and 4 freights.

Around 08.00 every day, the loco shed coal shunt was done. This entailed bringing loaded wagons from the loco yard into the station, then propelling them as fast as possible up the steep incline to the high level coal stage. Known to us as 'the hump', it was a most impressive sight, the shunting engine going flat out. On the occasions they did not make it, they came back for a second try.

The topic of the former Signal School at Clapham - see Issue 7, commenced a thread that has continued since. Once of the contributors to the knowledge on the subject was Michael Harvey whose notes on the topic were published in Issue 11: pages 38-40. In consequence of that contribution we asked, "….. I don't suppose you would put pen to paper on your career as a signalman as well…..? We are delighted say he did with the enclosed result.
Still however some posts needed to make up the set….

(Photographs by John Scrace unless otherwise stated.)

Opposite top - Redhill 'B' dating from 1882 which replaced the first signal box here known as Red Hill Junction. This 1882 structure was itself originally Red Hill No 2 but had been renamed Redhill No 2 by 1932. The final name change, to that seen, occurred in 1956. the box survived until 12 May 1985. (The brick petticoat intended to afford some degree of protection against blast was a WW2 addition.)

Opposite bottom - 'W' class 2-6-4T No. 31914 on the 14.47 Norwood to Horsham, seen passing through the station on 25 July 1959.

Cleaning the box was another chore for us lads, a dust round and sweep up at the end of each shift of course, but the real work was done on Sunday mornings when the floor and pulling board in front of the levers was scrubbed: the latter had to be white. In addition, the windows were cleaned outside. Evening time was when the windows were cleaned on the inside and the considerable amount of brass polished.

Redhill 'B' was worked by four signalmen and two lads. The signalmen worked the usual early, late, and night turns, plus a 09.00 to 17.00 shift. This pattern meant that each boy worked mostly with just two of the men on a regular basis. My own pair were Jimmie Iddenden, himself a former booking boy at 'B' box, and Les Hillier, who came to the railway from the merchant navy.

It was Jimmie who encouraged me to learn the frame after about a year or so. Strictly speaking this was not allowed, but it was good practice for when you became a signalman yourself. Eventually and when on late turn, I would work the frame from 7 o'clock onwards until going off duty about 21.45, Jimmie in the meanwhile did the booking. There was no booking done at night.

At first I struggled with the signal and point levers, not appreciating how heavy some would be. Likewise I went through the process of hurting my fingers trying to pull levers held by an electric front lock, or the mechanical interlocking, but it made you learn. From time to time I worked with relief men. I particularly remember Maurice Skinner, a contributor to railway magazines, and the author of a book on Croydon's railways. There was also Harry Franklin, who had been a signalman at Horley in the 1920s: he would reminisce about the times steam trains would drop off slip coaches there as well as the sidings being full of horseboxes on the Gatwick race days.

Towards the end of 1961 I was looking for a signalman's position. Adult jobs began at 20 on BR at that time, but some low-grade Signalman's posts could be filled on an 'acting' basis by anyone a year or two younger. I learned that three vacancies had arisen at Dorking Town: a friend, Dick Budgen told me he had applied for a job there and suggested I did the same. Dorking was about halfway between Redhill and Guildford and despite being on an important route, was graded at a Class 4 - the lowest. (Grades were calculated by an assessment of the amount of work done on the 'marks' system, one mark per lever pulled or phone call,etc.)

A couple of weeks after applying, I had a visit from the Signal Inspector. "You've applied for Dorking", he said, "Can you do this job?" – meaning Redhill 'B'. I was wondering how to reply: to admit I could would mean I had broken the rules by operating the box, but to say no would hardly help my case and

On 31 July 1964, No. 31405 had charge of the 07.27 Reading South to Redhill seen waiting to leave Dorking Town. The coaching stock set, No. 264 is a Bulleid 3-car set, one of three then allocated to Reading - Tonbridge line services. This set number had in previous years been allocated to a 6-car rake.

Just a few weeks later and diesel power has appeared on a similar working. D6548 at the head of the 16.04 Redhill to Reading South. Dorking Town signal box can be seen alongside the train. 22 September 1964. Steam however, would remain the mainstay of passenger workings until finally superseded by the 3R 'tadpole' units.

thus imply I knew nothing about the practicalities of working a signal box. Before I could decide, Harry Franklin, who was relieving that day, gave a suitable response. This was in words that cannot be used here, but what was said left the Inspector in no doubt about my capabilities. Everyone laughed, the tension was broken and with that I felt reasonably confident I might get the job.

Indeed this was confirmed a few weeks later, when after interview with Mr Roberts, the Divisional Traffic Manager - who later came to be associated with the Bluebell Railway, I commenced a preliminary two week course in February 1962 at the Clapham signal school. After this, it was to Dorking itself for eight weeks practical learning with a last week at Clapham for revision and the final exam. Despite having passed, I then had another short wait for the signalling inspector to pass me on the actual box working, plus a run-through on the rules and local instructions. There was then the necessary paperwork to be completed to prove I was considered competent: I was a signalman at last.

Dorking Town was a 24-hour box, except on Sundays. I had two colleagues, my friend Dick Budgen and David Luck, who came from Deepdene, the former SR wartime headquarters but then still being used as offices by BR. He joined Dick and myself in the early months of 1962. We were all about the same

age and had all passed out within a few weeks of each other. It must have been fairly uncommon to have three men so young in the same box: at the time we were all under twenty.

The layout at Dorking Town was typical of that for a South Eastern wayside station, staggered platforms, and sash window signal box dating back to the 1860s. There were 32 levers in this rather quaint frame, much shorter than normal and consequently with less travel than the Westinghouse type I was familiar with. Between each lever were wooden blocks: removing one of these one day, I found a lost teaspoon - it stirred my tea until I retired.

Block working was with standard 3-position instruments. There were the normal three stop signals on each line, plus distants, and an intermediate home and distant on the down. These latter signals were power worked semaphores, while the up distant was a 2-aspect colour light. All other signals and points were manually operated. Not surprisingly, the hardest pull was that of the down distant, nearly a mile away on the Redhill side of Deepdene station. Here the trick in getting the arm to the 'off', was to pull the lever over as hard as possible, then ease it back an inch or two so bringing the arm to about a 'half off'. Next get the wire as tight as possible using the wire adjuster, ease the lever back and finally give another huge pull! Just as I had got used it, after a few months it too was replaced by a colour light!

The box at Dorking was quite large in relation to the size of frame, which left room for some creature comforts. The frame faced towards the running lines, so a chair, table, cupboard and desk were positioned along the rear wall where there was also a coal-fired kitchen range for cooking and heat. This latter item we used to clean with powdered black lead. It was a filthy job to do, but the range really shone afterwards. Lighting was by gas, as it was at the station, and with no running water, we had to use a can from the station.

While the Redhill to Guildford route was no main line, it was certainly an important secondary route . Eighteen passenger trains each way called on weekdays, two of them starting and terminating at Dorking. One of them, the 18.16 Guildford berthed in the down siding overnight. The remaining train was the through Wolverhampton to the south coast, summer only service, which passed through at high speed behind its regular 'Schools' class locomotive.

We also had around about 20 freight workings per day, of which the 06.00 Norwood to Guildford called to the station coal yard, situated behind the down platform and signal box. There was also a daily Woking to Tonbridge and return, conveying ballast from Meldon,, destined for use on the south eastern division.

The switchback nature of the line made life difficult for the crews of these freight trains. The usual practice was to run fast downhill to keep away from the following train as well as to gain sufficient impetus for the next ascent. With just a few vacuum-braked wagons at the front as a fitted head, these trains would come tearing down the banks at 60 mph or more, the engine still pulling to keep the couplings tight, while the guard had his own handbrake screwed down hard to keep the couplings taut: this gave rise to a trail of smoke and sparks after dark. I once had a waiting passenger rush up to the box in alarm after seeing one such train go by! I tried to reassure him that it was quite normal but I don't think he was convinced.

Running downhill from Betchworth to Deepdene, the line then rose at 1 in 96 to the summit at Westcott, midway between Dorking and Gomshall, the summit being marked by an overbridge known to generations of railwaymen as the 'welcome bridge'. From time to time hard-pressed steam engines would fail to make it and assistance had to be given, often even by a following passenger train.

A point to remember in emergency situations on this hilly route was the location of the many catch points. We had three on the down line through Dorking. For example, the first was at the foot of the gradient just beyond Deepdene, the next just past the advance starting signal, and the last almost at the summit - beyond the intermediate home. I once had a freight run back over the second set, but then get on the move again, although derailing a wagon in the process. This it then dragged along until reaching the final set of catch point where it miraculously re-railed itself!

Diesel traction in the form of the Class 33 'Cromptons' arrived in the summer of 1963, the all-steam show was now over.

At this stage, the diesels were confined to the freight duties, no doubt to ensure both familiarity and reliability were obtained. The 'Cromptons' would later became one of the most reliable diesel classes on BR, but it was certainly not so in their early years when hauling heavy freights up the steep grades. This would cause them to overheat at which point the engine would automatically shut down. Several times I remember a class 33-hauled freight drifting down from Wescott to come to a stop outside the box with the driver declaring it a failure.

Dorking town was far from being a major centre, but it was still quite active in its own way. Passengers were fewer than at Deepdene – which was better placed for most, but parcels and mail traffic were quite heavy, the railway and British Road Services lorries calling each morning to collect their respective loads, while the GPO met most trains, including the last down Reading at night.

Horses were also regularly dealt with, at least in my first year or so. They were loaded or unloaded in a short dock at the Redhill end of the down platform. In those days we thought nothing of delaying a passenger train by up to ten minutes to shunt the engine over to pick up a horsebox, or perhaps even set the complete train back into the siding - that was in the case of down trains. Empty horse boxes were returned on the local freight. I also recall the Deepdene House messenger coming round twice a day in his small minibus to collect any correspondence destined for the offices.

The coal yard behind the box was busy with merchant's lorries coming and going. This was accompanied by the crash as the coal wagon doors were opened, followed by a roar as tons of coal fell into the pens accompanied by a cloud of coal dust drifting upwards into the air.

The station, in spite of its name, was situated on the edge of the town and undeveloped country lay to the west. As the line climbed up through the North Downs, it was possible in the still of the evening, to hear a train arrive at Gomshall, start away up the bank and follow it by sound all the way to Dorking, a distance of about 5 miles. When on the night shift during the summer, I would sometimes sit on the box steps with a cup of tea, watching the sun rise over Box Hill – delightful.

At night I would be on my own of course, although during the day there were staff on duty at the station. A leading porter worked the early and late turn and another porter on a middle turn. Our stationmaster was based at Dorking North, but paid a regular visit each day.

Despite its patronage and use, the route through Dorking Town was set out for closure in the Beeching report. Fortunately for once the local management rebelled and began to develop the line with diesel units made up from ex-Hastings line sets. This would lead to it becoming the busy route it remains today.

I have dealt at some length with my time at Dorking, but it laid the foundation of my career. We had to be capable of handling everything that happened, including dealing with other staff, often with years more experience than ourselves. Most railwaymen, though, were always very helpful to us youngsters.

Opposite top - *The 15.04 Redhill to Reading South at Dorking Town in charge of No. 31866, 22 September 1964.*
Opposite bottom - *A few minutes later and the same train is captured leaving the station: the fireman too seemingly also little altered from his previous pose. Perhaps it was to enquire if the smoke effect was exactly what had been requested!*

The second signal box at Merstham dating from September 1906. Originally equipped with a 21 lever frame, this was extended to 27 levers in 1940. These additional six levers were added at the south end of the frame and already had numbers stamped into the handles that bore no resemblance to anything at Merstham. This addition of second hand equipment was warranted by having to control the down yard connections installed at this time and intended to relieve congestion at the Redhill yards.

Due to the switchback nature of the line referred to, I was often invoking the various rules and regulations set up to deal with out of course events. Indeed I was once told by a station inspector at Redhill, that Dorking was the place to go to learn, as I would get through every rule in the book! I think I probably did, including weeks of single line working for a bridge renewal.

There were also some difficult shunt moves at times. On my first Saturday night I had an engineer's train working that involved running round the train, reversing the brake van, reversing the fitted head, and then dividing the train between up and down lines. Dorking was certainly interesting, but I had to move on and in 1964 obtained a Class 3 post at Merstham so returned to the main line again.

Merstham was yet another former SER box, this time with a brick lower floor rather than the all wood construction of Dorking. It had an Evans O'Donnell frame of 27 levers, again controlling the usual three signals each way, plus distants. All were semaphore excepting the down distant. The points were mechanically worked, except for two sets at the south end which gave access to the down yard.

Evans O'Donnell frames looked similar to the Westinghouse except for one nasty difference - for the signalman that is. When pulling a lever, the trigger (-sometimes referred to as the 'catch-handle') would come back hard against the lever handle when in mid-travel, a nasty trap for the fingers.

Sykes instruments, with their noisy track treadles for each signal, were still in use, although we also had a number of track circuits. Again this was a 24 -hour box , but the boxes either side, Star Bridge and Holmethorpe closed at night. We then worked with Coulsdon North and Redhill 'A'. When Holmethorpe was open, the block section was very short, consequently trains were offered on to Star Bridge immediately they had been offered to us by Holmethorpe. Even to Star Bridge the section time was only two minutes, to Redhill it was the same.

At Merstham, a small coal yard on the upside was still open, but the main freight activity took place in the down yard, situated between the station and quarry lines. This held over 250 wagons and was used to keep empty sand wagons for the local sand quarry, reached by a steeply graded siding from Holmethorpe . There were about six trips a day, taking empties in and loaded vehicles out to Redhill for sorting and thence onward travel all over the country. I recall Warrington in particular as one place that was supplied.

For working the sidings, the procedure was for the sand company to first inform the booking office of the wagons required for each train, the clerk would then tell me and I then had to tell the train crew when they arrived. Our empties arrived on the 06.00 Norwood, and we had to keep a record of all wagons arriving and leaving on an up-to-date yard chart.

Occasionally engineering work or an emergency would close the quarry line so sending all main line trains via Redhill. When this happened, available line capacity, even working the short sections could not cope. We would give out of section to the box in rear and the next train was offered on and in section immediately, so indicating the following train had been waiting at the section signal. In these conditions it was quite usual to have three trains on each line at a time, one in the advance section, another waiting on the up advance starter, and a third approaching the up home. It was the same situation on the down line.

I cannot leave Merstham without a mention of my two colleagues there, Laurie, at the time nearing retirement who had been a signalman in the Horley / Gatwick area during the war. He told me of the time he walked from Gatwick to Horley during an air raid and had to take shelter under the steps of the still existing footbridge because of shrapnel falling from the sky. My other colleague, Brian Killick had been a booking lad with me at Redhill. We were to have periods of working together, on and off, for the next 40 years.

My new box at Redhill 'A' was a 1941-built Southern structure, often described as in the 'Odeon' style. Within was a

Redhill 'A' dating from 15 June 1941. As referred to in the text, the box contained a 40 lever frame, surprisingly smaller than the 53 lever frame installed in the box it had replaced.

40 lever Westinghouse frame which controlled the London end of the station. This included the five running lines and up yard reception road, the whole converging into double track. There was also a GPO dock siding serving the adjacent sorting depot as well as two long up and down sidings.

Redhill 'A' was a great improvement over the old SER boxes I been used to. The design with its angled end windows reduced reflection at night, while the rear-positioned frame gave easy access to the front windows necessary for train observation. As structures, these boxes were built like castles with 18-inch-thick solid brick walls. If they had a weakness it was the flat roof which tended to leak unless treated regularly

The work was also not greatly different to that which I had experienced a few years earlier: true the steam engines had gone, but diesel locos and units still berthed in the old depot. Freight traffic may also have reduced but the local sand traffic was still considerable. This, together with more engineers' trains and use of the sidings for some van trains kept the yard staff fairly busy.

The infamous 'Tadpole' units worked most of the branch services, though some turns were covered by 'Crompton' hauled 3-car sets. Probably the biggest change was in the vast increase in mail and parcels traffic. Some was carried by passenger train, but much more by scheduled van trains. Some of these started or terminated at Redhill, others used the station as a staging point with vans attached or removed. Several of these workings had run for years, one being the regular Dover TPO. We also had at least two regular separate morning newspaper workings, one for Brighton and the other to Eastbourne.

To cope with all this van traffic, we had a diesel station pilot based at the 'A' box end, where most of the shunting took place. This engine also dealt with the remaining loco-hauled stock and was at work almost 24 hours a day. Indeed so heavy was the van traffic, that it could not all be handled in the mail dock and had to be unloaded in the down platform between trains, we even had authority to shunt into the platforms behind passenger trains, and did so all the time. At this period Redhill had about 330 trains daily, but over double that number of shunt movements.

Christmas time was unbelievable, mail bags stacked to the roof and so close to the platform edge it was almost unsafe to walk along it. We had at least one occasion when passengers were overcarried, claiming they were unable to open the doors due to the press of mailbags. To deal with the influx, extra staff were taken on, a number of relief signalmen acting as supervisors. Relief stationmasters were also brought in, working shifts round the clock, to try and keep some sort of order. So great was the workload that an additional loco pilot was provided. This shunted the south end of the station, whilst some passenger services were diverted via the quarry line all to give platform capacity for the additional mail trains. As an idea to the volume of these trains, we normally had around 20 van trains on a weekday, a figure which would double at Christmas. Despite all the careful planning I will admit it did sometimes collapse in chaos with consequent heavy delays to other trains. In those days Redhill station was full of life, the rumble of the GPO overhead conveyer belt, the clatter of trolleys along the platform and the shouts of the postmen and railmen humping mailbags – plus the sound of the diesel shunters coming and going - all combined to present a picture of continuous activity so absent today.

One obvious problem was where to put all these vans. Not only were both yards used, but we were given special authority to berth them on the through lines as well. This hectic activity would last for about three weeks and then come Christmas Eve, it was all over, the station would empty and all be quiet again.

Despite the increase in one type of traffic, other freight was rapidly in decline. So much so that by the mid-1970s most of the freight dealt with at Redhill was engineers' workings. Several of these ran each day between Woking and the large p/way depot at Three Bridges. Similar trains operated between Woking and Tonbridge. There was also a spent ballast tip at Godstone,

Left - The up line starting signals at Redhill, controlled from 'A' box in the background.

Bottom - 'D1' No. 31487 on the 15.12 Redhill to Tonbridge service awaiting departure from Redhill, 18 July 1959. The coaching set No. 213, was originally one of four similar sets built in 1929 for London - Bexhill - Hastings line trains.

served from both Three Bridges and Woking, both of which involved the engines of these train running round at Redhill.

Later, when construction of the M23 and M25 was under way. depots were set up at Gatwick and Merstham to receive roadstone. This arrived via the Guildford – Redhill and meant another change of direction. Several trains ran each day plus a nightly Lydd to Mersham trip. Some of these stone workings had Western Region 'Warship' diesels in charge: some of their last duties before withdrawal.

Local sand traffic from Merstham Quarry was still heavy at this stage, often running seven days a week. All these various freight and ballast workings could combine to cause se-vere congestion on occasions. Indeed I recall times when all three platform roads, both through lines and the yard reception were simultaneously occupied by freight trains - a most impressive sight.

While there were no bi-directional running lines at Redhill, trains could start back from the up platforms. All lines were though reversible for shunt moves. However, at 'A' box end, the layout allowed for two right line and two wrong line movements into the station at the same time: thus four trains running parallel on adjoining lines. In my twelve years at 'A' box I managed it twice!

The 152 lever box at Three Bridges, another BR structure dating from 1952. In its final days, it was re-branded 'Three Bridges ASC' wef 25 June 1963, although it is doubtful if this name was other than a paper exercise as the box closed on 2 July 1983.

A number of changes took place in the box during those 12 years too. The track layout was slightly altered and a number of the points converted to power operation. To reflect the changes, the old SR illuminated diagram was replaced by a modern version. This new diagram was drawn and coloured to a much higher standard than the old version, and I thought was a real work of art.

The old Walker's train describers were also by now worn out and somewhat unreliable, leading to false descriptions and consequently the wrong route being set up. We made numerous complaints, and eventually new magazine type describers were installed throughout from Coulsdon North to Earlswood. These had 24 different descriptions so gave more precise information.

During the 1970s there was a change in how signalboxes were graded and similarly how they were assessed. Under the new scheme Redhill 'A' became a 'Class D', the same as 'B' box. As previously recounted, in the past 'B' had been a 'Special A' – one step higher than we were. One advantage with the new scheme was that men in class 'Class D' and above were given establishment status with enhanced salary and membership of the superior salaried pension fund.

In my time at Redhill, 'A' box had become like a second home, as I had spent so much of my waking hours at work. But nothing is permanent, and in 1978 a vacancy was advertised at Three Bridges, my home town. My application was successful and several months later I found myself learning another new box.

Three Bridges was also a 'Class D', so the move was only a transfer rather than promotion, but about a year later we had our marks taken again and were regraded as a 'Class E', so I got my promotion after all.

The box here dated from 1951 and was another Odeon-style building but on an even more massive scale. There were also single-storey extensions at each end which gave accommodation for the relay room and S & T mess rooms and workshop.

Entering at ground level, one first came into a hallway where doors to left and right led to the locking room and the S & T quarters. Immediately in front was access to the boiler room, stairs to upper floor and toilet: yes, an indoor toilet at last. In fact the box had been designed so that most areas were accessible without going outside, the relay room being the major exception.

A Westinghouse A3 frame had been installed when built, at 152 levers it was also the largest mechanical frame on the Southern. We controlled a mix of multiple-aspect signalling on the main line, with semaphore signals and block working on the two branches to Crawley and Rowfant. There was a similar mix of power and mechanical operated points.

By the time of my arrival big changes had taken place. The East Grinstead branch had closed and the associated sidings lifted, except that for the former bay platform, still used for berthing the odd loco. MAS had also been introduced on the Horsham line, so removing the last of the semaphore signals. All the points were also converted to power operation, the final few sets soon after my arrival.

Three Bridges had once been an important freight marshalling centre, but such work had gone by this time. None the less, a fair amount of activity still took place in both the up and down yards, as a major track depot had been established in the up yard and engineers trains ran to all parts of the Central Division, especially at weekends. The site of the former steam shed was occupied by a tamper servicing depot

Consequent upon the reductions to the layout, a large number of levers had become spare, thus a few years before my arrival, the frame was shortened to 126 levers. This left room at one end for a route-setting panel to be installed to take over control of Gatwick Airport and replaced the former 75 lever LB&SCR box there, which had dated from the time of the former racecourse. Gatwick 'box was quickly demolished to allow for new station development. Around the same time Balcombe Tunnel Junction signal box was closed, its signals and points put on to spare levers in our frame.

Apart from any obvious economy, this was a sensible move from an operating perspective, as by controlling the junction from two tracks to four onwards at Three Bridges, it gave us greater flexibility in the regulation of up trains.

Three Bridges was staffed by three men on each shift, plus a signal lad who worked during the daytime. One of the three men looked after the Gatwick panel and the other two the frame. As was the nature of railway work where men move around to gain promotion, I already knew most of my new colleagues although I had to learn both the mechanical frame and the panel as we rotated in the actual box work.

As before, in due course I was passed out by the signalling inspector, a man I had first met when he himself had been a relief signalman 30 years earlier. Indeed he had sometimes relieved me at Dorking Town. Like many men of his generation and position, his working knowledge was considerable.

In 1980 work began on the Three Bridges resignalling scheme. This would eventually take over the main line from Brighton as far as Norbury and Anerly together with a good mileage of the connecting branches. Again there were changes to the frame, sometimes of short duration. Meanwhile the 'new works' S & T' people had taken over the down yard, temporarily increasing the work there to such extent that they required an additional shunter and engine

By 1982 steelwork for the new box was going up and our days were numbered. Located on the site of the former East Grinstead branch sidings, the new structure was directly in front of us, so we had a good view of progress. The reliable Westinghouse company had secured the contract for the signalling: their third visit to Three Bridges in 50 years, having put in the original MAS for the 1933 electrification. The structure of the main building was put up by a local firm, Longley's, who had an established record of railway work having been involved in railway structures in the south of England since the 1880s.

The end came in 1983. I, together with my colleagues had managed to obtain posts in the new box, again a promotional move as the new box was a 'Class F', the highest grade in the system. Thus I left mechanical levers behind, never to pull one again: the world of electronic control is another story.

Looking back on my 42 years, the most interesting period was without doubt the earlier times when steam was still active. During my time as booking boy I must have seen perhaps 30 different types of steam engine: not all were regular visitors, whilst at busy times engines would congregate on the through lines, then trundle off to the shed coupled together: three engines coupled in like fashion was common. At times it might be as many as five. They might all even represent different companies.

The end of steam coincided with the disappearance of other things as well, the closure of the local goods yards and the decline of wagon load freight. A study of freight traffic handled at Redhill was an education in British industry, what came from where and where it was going. Motor cars from the midlands to Dover destined for export, house coal from south Wales, biscuits from Reading, and gas coal for High Brooms. Incoming might be ferry vans from Dover, huge rolls of paper from Sittingbourne, cement from Snodland, and even power station slack from Kent to the London area, just some of the variety on offer.

The closing stages of the 1960s also saw the end of the dreadful fogs which so blighted railway working years before. None of the lines I worked on then had the Automatic Warning System installed, yet in spite of this, I never had a train pass a red signal in fog. Fogmen were stationed at the more strategic signals, but calling them out in the days when few people had phones was difficult. It was the tradition of the railway that under such conditions, many men would arrive of their own accord, assuming they would be wanted.

Progress in the installation of colour light signals meant that fogmen were not required: one reason why so many semaphore distants were replaced around this time and not just because the levers were a hard pull for the signalman! I can still vividly recall hanging out of the window of Redhill 'A' listening for a sound: a coupling dropping for instance, which would tell you what was going on.

A signalman worked with many other people of course, train crews and station staff being the most obvious. At a busy station like Redhill where shunting was a regular activity, we were in almost constant communication with the station inspector, shunters, and yard staff. To save on a phone call, visual signs were sometimes used. First we would get a blast on the horn from the pilot to attract our attention, then, on looking out, the driver would be leaning out of his cab with two fingers above his head like horns: this meant he wanted the cattle dock. There were also several others.

A daily visitor to the box was the stationmaster, always signing the book to prove his presence, as did the signalling inspector on his less frequent calls. P/way men would also appear from time to time, particularly if track possession was to be taken. Then the S & T staff would turn up to carry out maintenance, or attend to a failures - and how glad were we to see them if a failure had us badly locked up!

Building department workers sometimes came to carry out jobs on the building or the utility services. Indeed during my time at Redhill 'A' we had to have a new water supply installed when the original became contaminated.

Perhaps the most interesting of the specialist technical staff were the locking fitters, both mechanical and electrical. Redhill S & T had their own mechanical fitter, but the electric locks and controllers were dealt with by two fitters from Wimbledon. The older of the two, Alec, had begun his career in the 1940s and claimed to have worked at every box on the Southern, plus a few taken over from the Western. He could also remember all the various types of frame they had.

Opposite top - Special working at Three Bridges, 22 March 1964. 'N'. Class 2-6-0, No. 31411 arrives with the joint LCGB / RCTS 'Sussex Downsman' tour. Five different locos were used for this train, which had commenced from Waterloo and would eventually arrive back at Victoria, via: Epsom, Guildford, Horsham, Steyning, Hove, Three Bridges, Tunbridge Wells West, Heathfield, Pevensey, Lewes, Brighton, Kemp Town, Uckfield and Oxted.

Opposite bottom - The more usual working on the Tunbridge Wells West trains in the mid 1960s. No. 80018 setting of from three Bridges on 12 May 1965. Passenger services on this line closed from 1 January 1967.

His opposite number came from Italy, and by repute made the best tea on the railway. It was a real art with him, making sure the water was fresh and having the correct amount of ingredients.

I should say that I was never directly involved with any serious mishap on the main line, although I did once have an electric unit run away from Three Bridges on the up fast during the early hours, eventually coming to rest in Horley.

Minor derailments, or collisions were common when shunting and I witnessed a fair number of these. Most were caused by simple means, for instance a driver propelling a long train might lose sight of the shunter or perhaps not even be able to see which road his movement was going into. Or vehicles which were left in a dark siding without a tail lamp at night, or a light which had gone out, were then hit. Sometimes too a signalman could misjudge the position of a movement in the dark and pull over a set of points underneath a vehicle - that is if they were not locked by track circuit, and many siding points were not!

My abiding memory of this sort of error, was of poor old Matt, the carriage and wagon fitter at Redhill. There he was, sat underneath a bogie van which had been pushed over the stops in the mail dock, surrounded by his collection of jacks and packing, trying to work out how to get it back on the track. One buffer had ridden over the buffer beam of the stops, the other had gone underneath and sideways, in the process becoming wedged below the timber platform of the dock. How he did it I never saw, but all was in order the next day, though the evidence was there for all to see in that that the timber platform had taken a bashing!

Above - Reading based former SECR 'D' class No. 31075 at Redhill circa 1951/52.   Arthur Tayler

Opposite page - "My interest in steam engines began in the mid-30s at the age of about twelve, when my father took me on occasions to the roundhouse loco shed at Horsham, where he was part of the engine maintenance staff. These visits were often arranged when routine exams were taking place on their various engines based at the depot, so giving me the chance to see engines in stripped down condition. There were about forty engines at the depot at the time. I can recall the following engines and numbers from those times: Two 'K' Class Nos. 2345 & 2348, four Marsh Goods Nos. 2300, 2301, 2306 & 2307, four C2X Nos. 2449, 2521, 2522 & 2550, two E5Xs (Tanks) Nos. 2401 & 2570, several E5 Tanks, several E4 Tanks, incl. Nos. 2464, 2511 & 2515, two E-Type shunters Nos. 2138 & 2149, several D3s incl. Nos. 2373, 2365, 2384 & 2387, three or four D1s incl. Nos. 2235 & 2252. From 1942, seven Maunsell Q Class were added – nos. 540 to 547. The D3s & D1s were replaced in the early 1950s by Drummond M7 Tanks, nos. 30047 to 30053. The shed had eighteen roads, each of which could hold two tanks, as many were berthed that way on Sundays. Soon after my seventeenth birthday my father arranged for me to be interviewed by the shedmaster at Horsham where I was given the post of cleaner, subject to an A1 medical. After about two years of cleaning, or being upgraded to fireman when required, I was appointed as a fireman, where I progressed through the various links until 1948 when I was passed for driving. Being a passed fireman, though mostly driving for five years, I secured the post of driver at Three Bridges in 1953. Returning to Horsham in 1955 I joined the dual link which comprised a mix of steam and electric duties (E.M.U.T.) where I remained until 1959. When a vacancy occurred in the Motorman's panel at Horsham I left steam for good finally retiring in December 1987. The photograph of the Terrier and myself was taken in Brighton loco yard in 1955 after completion of my E.M.U.T. training."   J G Brooker

THE LONGEST PASSENGER TRAIN EVER TO ARRIVE AT HORSHAM?

Jack Brooker, with thanks also to Paul Kear

During my spell as a fireman at Horsham locomotive depot I was required to act as second man on the electric locos which our depot were rostered to work.

One afternoon in November 1947, Driver D. Weatherall and I were scheduled to work a goods train from Horsham to Norwood with electric loco No. CC1. By the time of our departure, freezing rain was settling on everything including the conductor rail, causing delays to all trains, which meant our pathway was lost and our trip cancelled. Being told to await further orders we watched various electric trains trying to make headway, giving a display of flashing and arcing all evening. We were then recalled to the depot about 10.00 pm, having left our loco berthed.

The depot Foreman explained that some trains were stranded and needing assistance, with the nearest being just north of Faygate. We took Q Class No. 543 to Faygate station where we were crossed over to the down line, to go north ¾-mile to the stranded train.

It transpired that the twelve-car "Nelson", the 6.08 pm from Victoria to Bognor, had got into trouble after leaving Three Bridges. The following train (also a twelve-car Nelson) from London Bridge to Portsmouth was sent to assist the first one. These two trains struggled to Ifield where they were given help

from the rear by an E4 Class steam loco but which was then beaten by the rising gradient near Faygate. The time was now about 11.00 pm and with both buffet cars also empty of stock, some passengers had left the trains to cross the fields to the main A264 road to reach Horsham.

On coupling our engine to the leading motor coach I was advised by the Motorman that his compressors were able to maintain brake pressure, while if we did the pulling, he would operate the brakes: the Q Class only fitted for vacuum brake working.

After exchanging whistles, as per the rule book for assisting engines (two crows), we were able to move the train of twenty-four coaches to the level gradient at Faygate, from where the gradient falls to Horsham, arriving about twenty minutes later. At 24 vehicles, probably the longest service passenger train to arrive at Horsham.

Here the rear twelve coaches were taken off as the motors had burnt out. The front Motorman though required our assistance further, which meant us continuing tender-first calling at stations to Arundel, where the icing was not as severe.

From there on, the Motorman decided he could manage, so I uncoupled our engine and we returned light engine to Horsham so ending a duty of about eleven hours.

EXTRACTS FROM THE SOUTHERN RAILWAY TRAFFIC CONFERENCE MINUTES

Compiled by David Monk-Steel

5235. (21 June 1926) TRAFFIC RECEIPTS

Submitted:- The following statement of Traffic Receipts for the six weeks ending 13 June 1926, as compared with the corresponding period in 1925:-

	1926	1925	Increase	Decrease	
Miles open	2,183	2,153	30	-	%
Passenger Train Goods Train	£ 1,478.000 379,000	£ 2,061,000 668,000	£ - -	£ 583,000 289,000	28.28 43.26
Totals £	1,857,000	2,729,000	-	872,000	32
Aggregate for 26 weeks: -	£	£	£	£	%
Passenger Train Goods Train	6,404,999 2,392,000	6,874,000 2,656,000	- -	470,000 264,000	7 10
Totals	£ 8,796,000	£ 9,530,000	£ -	£ 734,000	8

Note - General and Coal Strike, 1926.

5427. (22 November 1926) RESERVATION OF SEATS IN TRAINS

Reported:- That as from Monday, 15 November, arrangements have been made whereby intending passengers may have seats reserved at a fee of 1s. Per seat in the 11.00 a.m. train from Waterloo with portions for Ilfracombe, Torrington, Plymouth, Padstow, Bude, Exmouth and Sidmouth, and in the 12.30 p.m. train from Waterloo with portions for Weymouth, Swanage and Bournemouth, also in the return services at the following times, viz: -

Ilfracombe	10.22 a.m.	Torrington	10.25 a.m.
Plymouth	10.15 a.m.	Padstow	8.35 a.m.
Bude	9.45 a.m.	Exmouth	11.40 a.m.
Sidmouth	12.10 p.m.	Weymouth	5.25 p.m.
Swanage	1.20 p.m.	Bournemouth West	6.18 p.m.

The seats in these trains will be numbered, the passengers being given a ticket bearing the number of the seat, etc., corresponding with labels which will be used by staff in making the reservations. In the event of its becoming necessary to attach vehicles in which seats are not numbered the passenger's name will be substituted for a number.

In addition to reservations made at the starting points, facilities will be given for a similar arrangement at various important intermediate stations en route, who will advise staff at the starting points as to the requirements.

So far as these trains are concerned, the new arrangement will supersede that under which compartments are now reserved at a fee of 5s.

(22 JUNE 1926) SIDCUP

At 3.30 p.m. smoke was seen to be issuing from the roof of the Station Master's house at Sidcup. An inspection was at once made by means of a ladder, when it was found that the fire was beyond the control of the Station Staff. The local Fire Brigade was therefore summoned, and arrived at 4.0 p.m., by which time the roof was well alight. The outbreak was extinguished at 5.30 p.m., but the top floor of the house was destroyed and the lower portion damaged by water. The Station Master's furniture, however, was removed from the house to the lawn before the arrival of the fire brigade.

The fire was attributed to a spark emitted from the engine of the 1.5 p.m. goods train from Northfleet to Hither Green. American coal was being burnt and the gradients are heavy.

The following new works are recommended:-

Station	Nature of Work	Nos. of Plans	Estimated Cost
Charing Cross, Waterloo Junction, Cannon Street and London Bridge	Abolition of existing direction boards and the erection of pedestal boards for information of passengers.	31,540. 31,541. 31,542. 31,543. 31,544	£376
East Guldeford Level crossing between Appledore and Rye	Provision of up and down distant signals together with ground frame and electrical repeaters.	30,714	£342
London Bridge (Eastern Section)	Raising of Platforms Nos. 5 and 6 to standard height and incidental alterations to the level of Platforms Nos. 4 and 7.	31,013. 31,014. 31,015	£1,925 (a)
London Road, Guildford	Provision of additional siding together with coal ground and roadway.	28,353	£1,955 (b)
Wareham	Removal of signal box from the western end to the eastern end of the station and placing crossing gates under control of signalman; provision of ground frame at the western end of the station; removal of existing ground frame at the eastern end to another site; abolition of the gatekeeper's hut, and extension of track circuits, etc.	24,172. 3,554	£3,139 (c)
Whitstable Harbour	Re-building of goods shed and stables and incidental alterations.	29,143	£1,850 (a)
Gravesend West Street Pier	Provision of electric crane and lighting of the station by electricity.	-	£1,175 (d)
Deal	Re-arrangement of Station offices on up platform. Demolition of wall at station entrance and substitution of iron fence.	30,752. 31,495	£437 (e)
Canterbury West	Re-arrangement of office accommodation on the up platform.	28,541	£1,000 (a)
Wilmington Level Crossing, between Polegate and Berwick	Provision of capstan wheel for working crossing gates from the Signal Box instead of from the ground frame.	-	£313

a.   To be charged to the Fund for re-building of Station.
b.   To be charged to Capital.
c.   Estimated saving of £396.10s.0d per annum in wages will be effected. To be charged to New Works Revenue Suspense Account.
d.   The Batavier Line will contribute £100, and an existing old 10-cwt hand crane will be dispensed with. £815 of the outlay should be charged to Capital.
e.   The re-arrangement will enable a saving of £230 per annum in staff to be effected.

5299. (24 JULY 1926) SIDING AT HAMWORTHY. APPLICATON OF POOLE HARBOUR BOARD

Referring to the Memorandum of Agreement dated 14 December, 1922, between the old London and South Western Company and the Machinery and Trading Corporation Limited, under which the latter were granted permission to use the siding at Hamworthy Quay, and Officers' Conference Minute 3568 dated 3 October, 1922, also an agreement dated 14 December, 1922, with the Poole Harbour Commissioners, at the time this permission was granted the Machinery and Trading Corporation were the sub-tenants of the Stanlee Shipbreaking and Salvage Company Limited, Lessees of the Poole Harbour Commissioners, but the lease having now expired the Poole Commissioners have granted a lease of the wharf to the Southern Roadways Limited, and in connection therewith, have requested the Company to grant the use of the siding to the Southern Roadways Limited, as was done in the case of the Machinery and Trading Corporation. It is recommended that the facility be granted under a proper document.

5817. (3 OCTOBER 1927) APPLICATION OF SOUTHERN ROADWAYS LIMITED, HAMWORTHY

Referring to Minute No. 5299, dated 26 July, 1926, in regard to the completion of an agreement with the Southern Roadways Limited, as to the user of the Poole Harbour Commissioners' Siding, at Hamworthy, application has now been made by the Firm for permission to make use of a Muir-Hill N.C. Type Standard Gauge Locomotive on the sidings in question. There is no objection to this, and it is recommended that the request be acceded to under a suitable supplemental agreement, relieving this Company of all liability in connection with such user, and also that the use of the locomotive shall not interfere with movements on this Company's sidings.

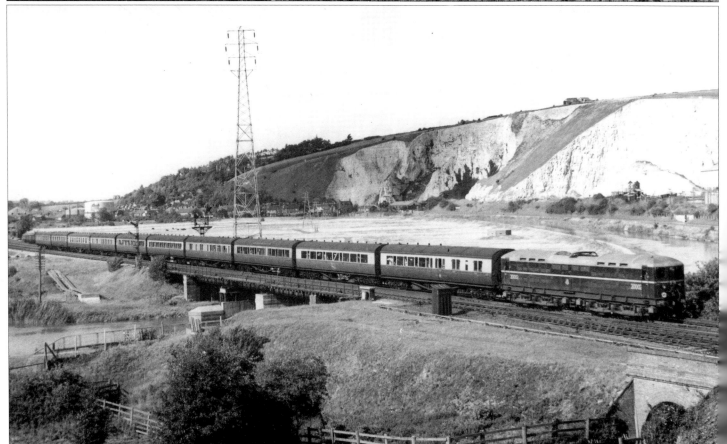

LEWES - RAILWAY MEMORIES

Derek Saunders

My earliest memories of the railway at Lewes are of lying in bed at night hearing the clash of buffers as wagons were shunted in the yard, about half a mile from where I then lived in Malling Street. I once read that a railway engineering institute was once located in the same street and apparently visited by many well known names in the railway world, including Maunsell and Gresley. Unfortunately, the actual building and several others of considerable architectural interest, were demolished in the 1970s to make way for the Phoenix Causeway bridge and associated road to by-pass the narrow Cliffe High Street. Locally, many people also believe this new road was the reason for the demise of the line between Lewes and Uckfield and for the simple reason that extra expense would have been needed to construct a bridge over the new road for the railway.

Shunting of goods trains at Lewes went on throughout the day and night as stock from the Eastbourne, Seaford, Uckfield, Brighton and London lines was sorted and remarshalled. Because of this interchange, Lewes possessed an extensive goods yard, the road entrance to which was from the High Street. In the '50s and '60s there was a regular train of Kellogg's cereals unloaded in a siding immediately to the east of the yard entrance and placed on to trailers drawn by Scammel Scarabs. The large cartons were then transported away to a local warehouse to await distribution.

Immediately adjacent to the entrance to the goods yard and passing over the High Street was the bridge carrying the Uckfield line. This line curved at about 90 degrees almost immediately after leaving Lewes station, rising on brick arches to the bridge over the High Street. It ran for most of its course parallel with the goods yard.

The bridge itself was quite a notable feature, as the sides were made of wood on a wooden framing. The underside was clad in corrugated iron but already somewhat buckled due to being regularly struck by high vehicles. A number of Southdown buses, and

Opposite top - 'K + K' at Southerham Junction. No. 32345 is in charge of the through Walsall to Hastings service, whilst opposing is No. 32344 with an up goods.
                                                    S C Nash

Opposite bottom - Southerham Bridge, Lewes. 'Hornby' No. 20002 on the last leg of the through Birmingham Snow Hill to Eastbourne service, 22 July 1950.
S C Nash

quite likely those from Maidstone & District which also passed through Lewes, had come to grief here over the years.

To return to the marshalling and goods yards. The lines that passed from the marshalling yard, some of which passed into the goods yard, also continued to curve round to the west back towards Lewes station, or at least, to the London side of the station. Part of this track formation had followed the course of the old route into the original Lewes station in Friars Walk, located adjacent to what became the goods yard. The original station building was a fine large building in the Italianate style, and whilst its life as a station was short, it was not finally demolished until the 1970s to make way for the local Law Courts. I don't remember it serving any purpose in my lifetime and although the windows on the side facing the road were bricked up and consequently appearing uncared for, it still retained an air of grandeur. Position-wise, it was extremely convenient for the town centre but, as it had been the terminus of the first line into Lewes from Brighton, when further expansion occurred, it was inconvenient to operate a station where a reversal was required for every

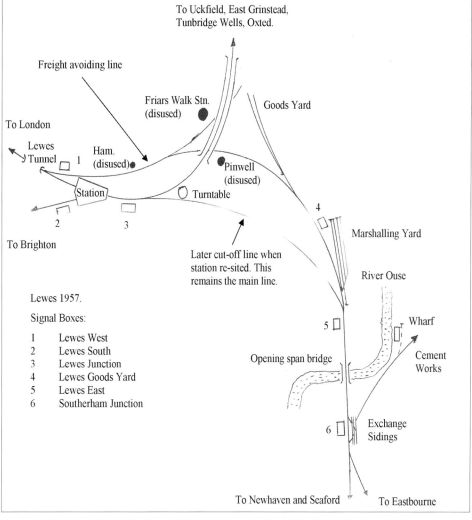

To Uckfield, East Grinstead,
Tunbridge Wells, Oxted.

Freight avoiding line

Friars Walk Stn.
(disused)

Goods Yard

To London

Lewes
Tunnel   Ham.
                (disused)   Pinwell
         1   (disused)

Station   Turntable

                                        4
         2   3   Marshalling Yard

To Brighton
                                        River Ouse

                Later cut-off line when
                station re-sited. This
                remains the main line.   5   Wharf

                                Opening span bridge   Cement
                                                             Works

Lewes 1957.

Signal Boxes:

1   Lewes West
2   Lewes South   6   Exchange
3   Lewes Junction   Sidings
4   Lewes Goods Yard
5   Lewes East
6   Southerham Junction

To Newhaven and Seaford   To Eastbourne

Gladstone class 0-4-2 leaving Platform 6 with a Brighton to Tunbridge Wells, via Uckfield, service, circa 1920.

'H2' No. 32426 Lewes, 5 July 1951. The service - London Bridge to Brighton, via Oxted and East Grinstead, is arriving at Lewes from from the Oxted line and seen crossing Lewes Junction .
R C Riley / The Transport Treasury

through movement. As a result the fascinating, albeit rather involved story of Lewes' various stations came about.

The tracks from the marshalling yard which continued beyond the goods yard, joined the London line close to the entrance to Lewes tunnel.

Controlling this junction was Lewes West signal box. This box contained an interesting green painted lever, the purpose of which was to ring a gong in Lewes goods yard and so to let them know a freight train was on its way. As the marshalling yard faced south, towards the Eastbourne and Seaford line direction, freight from and to the London line which required to call at Lewes, used this junction to access the yards. Trains from the Uckfield line similarly destined for the goods yard, had to continue into Lewes station, on to the London line and then pull forward into the tunnel, before reversing via this junction and round to the yard. Similarly trains destined for the Uckfield line would

need to reverse from the yards, into Lewes tunnel sometimes for quite a way, in order to take a run at the initial steep climb and sharp curve of the Uckfield line and across the bridge over the High Street.

As a boy I would sit on Cliffe Hill overlooking Lewes, the marshalling and goods yard, and, with the station in the middle distance, watch the activity. There were two regular shunting engines, E4s, I believe. Naturally there were also trains frequently passing on the 'new' direct main line, which curved round from the station, avoiding the old route via the goods yard, thence making a trailing junction with the marshalling yard and heading south towards Southerham Junction where the lines to Eastbourne and Seaford parted. Immediately before this junction the railway crossed the River Ouse on a bridge that, at one time, could be opened to allow the passage of small ships and sailing barges. This bridge was manually controlled and needed the ef-

With Brighton behind the camera, we are looking east to the point where the London, Uckfield and Southerham Junction (thereafter to Eastbourne or Seaford) lines converge opposite Lewes Junction Signal Box. From left to right, the platforms are Nos. 4/5, 6, 7, and 8. Nos, 4/5 and 6 were used by Uckfield, Seaford and Eastbourne trains, Brighton trains used Nos. 7 and 8. The carriage siding is to the far right. Lewes South (later 'D') signal box is visible in the bottom right hand corner. In the middle distance a train can be seen on the junction.

The Lens of Sutton Association

forts of 30 men to open it. Consequently when the main line was electrified in 1934, the Southern approached the nearby Eastwoods Cement Company, who had a wharf upstream of the bridge, with a view to making alternative arrangements for transporting their cement. An agreement was finally reached by which the Southern would transport the cement from the sidings at Southerham to Newhaven Harbour for transfer to shipping. This may well have been a free service by the SR, provided as an alternative to the need to open the bridge. Uncertainty thus exists as to whether any charge was ever made to the cement company for this service. What we do know is that as a result of this agreement, the last ship to leave Eastwood's wharf at Southerham was the M V 'Plymouth Trader' in November 1934, loaded with 155 tons of cement. The other obvious advantage to the Southern was in the removal of delays to traffic at this point.

However, despite this easing, the actual opening bridge still remained *insitu* with the railway legally bound to open it once a year in order to preserve the right to navigation. This arcane requirement persisted until the 1950s, and was really little different to numerous Private Roads up and down the land where to preserve their Private Road status they too were closed for one day a year – usually a bank holiday when usage would be small anyway. To return to the bridge over the River Ouse, sailing barges were still able to pass underneath by the simple expedient of lowering the mast, again as time passed so the use of such barges ceased altogether.

To the east side of Southerham Junction were a couple of sidings at which traffic for The Eastwood Cement works was dropped off and collected. I would imagine wagons were tripped from and to Lewes marshalling yard by one of the yard pilots. Certainly post steam and after the closure of the various yards at Lewes, wagons continued to be dropped off and collected by a loco, usually a class 73, which then continued on towards Newhaven either to run round or deal with more traffic.

Over the years Messrs. Eastwoods had various locos of their own to deal with the wagons at the sidings, drawing them the quarter of a mile or so to and from the works. One was an

Andrew Barclay 0-4-0ST saddle tank No. 919, another a Hawthorn Leslie 0-4-0ST saddle tank which carried the name 'Atlas', and finally Kerr Stuart No. 4247. In the final years before closure of the works in the 1980s, a small industrial diesel shunter was used. Subsequent to the closure of the cement works, the site was rejuvenated as an industrial estate. Quizzically, the last diesel shunter was left on a short section of track beside a car park serving the estate. It was quite a while before it disappeared.

Although the Lewes by-pass now overshadows the site of the exchange sidings, some rails can still be found in the concrete road leading towards the site of the cement works. This concrete though was itself fairly recent and only appeared in the latter days of the works, slightly to the south of the original compacted soil formation formerly used as the track bed. I well remember the creaks and groans as the little loco and its wagons slowly moved along the track. 'Atlas' especially seemed to heave its 'shoulders' from side to side as it pulled its load. Some trackwork may also still exist buried deep in the undergrowth alongside the main road into Lewes, the A26 south of the Cuilfail road tunnel.

The railway from the exchange sidings, crossed what was the main Lewes to Eastbourne road on a very sharp bend in the road and close by what was the now demolished 'Fox Inn'. A flagman would be employed to close the single barrier across the road whilst the train would cross to the sound of much whistling from the loco. I would imagine that, despite the relevant 'Ungated Level Crossing' sign, many a motorist coming from Eastbourne to Lewes still had a shock when rounding the bend.

Lewes station has seen a number of alterations over the years. Apart from the Uckfield line, which then made a junction with the East Grinstead line about three miles north of Lewes, all other passenger lines in Lewes were eventually electrified. With the electrification of the London line in the mid thirties, there was a need to extend the London line platforms to take twelve coach trains. As this was impossible at the south eastern end, due to the junction with the Brighton, Uckfield and Eastbourne / Seaford lines, the only alternative was towards the tunnel. It was there-

fore necessary to open out the southern end of the tunnel and re-align the avoiding lines - those which curved around to the goods and marshalling yards and were mentioned previously.

At one time, the line from Uckfield had entered Lewes from the London line and through Lewes tunnel. But when that line was realigned to approach the station via the route over the High Street, the old route via Hamsey was closed. Today the formation of the old line can still be seen curving away east from the London line near to Hamsey level crossing, to join the course of the Uckfield line beyond Hamsey village. The Uckfield line was closed to passengers in 1969, although freight continued for a short while afterwards. It is possible to pick up the course of this route towards Barcombe Mills and beyond, and also back towards Lewes, in places. As an aside, in the early 1960s, a 'Hornby' (Southern Electric loco) hauled boat train, demolished the gates at Hamsey Level crossing due to the crossing keeper not opening them in time.

If following the railway history of the area in practical terms, the more energetic can obtain a better view by taking a path to the left and on to the hill from Offham village, a couple of miles north of Lewes. Apart from the wonderful view of the countryside, there are two very fine hostelries back on the main road. One of these, the 'Chalkpit Inn', about a quarter of a mile back towards Lewes, is also of interest. It was the site of the first railway in Lewes, a simple expedient for getting chalk from the adjacent pit to the barges in the valley below. Built from the yard of the actual inn, two tunnels pass under the main road on a steep gradient that continues into the trees opposite to the bottom of the valley where a canal had been constructed from the nearby river Ouse. From the yard of the inn, although partly filled in, the tunnels are still visible, although the landlord does discourage further investigation. However, by looking over the wall on the opposite side of the road, it is possible to observe the exit from the tunnels. Apart from these tunnels, there is no trace of the trackwork down into the valley. The canal however still exists – just, but rather overgrown.

Opposite top - *Lewes Cement Works, 17 June 1962. 0-4-0ST 'Dolly', Kerr Stuart No. 4247 of 1922 at work.*

Opposite bottom - *Seen from the rear of the junction signal box in the last years of the works, circa 1966, after a diesel loco had taken over. Here the loco positions empty coal wagons in the exchange sidings at Southerham Junction prior to collecting the full wagons behind. Part of the pointwork for the divergence of the Eastbourne and Seaford lines can be seen in the bottom left hand corner. In recent years the actual junction has been moved further south.*

Above - *Southerham Junction, circa 1966. In the centre the works locomotive leaves the exchange sidings with loaded coal wagons. The actual cement works in the background. The wharf is on the outside curve of the River Ouse: above the bushes to the left of the loco. The opening bridge is just out of camera on the extreme left. The divergence of the coast line and Newhaven route is similarly just off camera to the right. Lewes station and yards are approximately half a mile from this location.*

Opposite page, top - *The view of the Keymer line platform and the West (later 'A')Signal Box. Lewes tunnel is behind the photographer. Under normal conditions, this signal box controlled the main and station avoiding lines.*

Opposite page, middle - *The usual electric service: compare the lever of water on the ground signal in this and the lower view.*
Lens of Sutton Association.

Opposite page, bottom - *BR Class 4 tank, No. 80153, operating the emergency steam replacement service between Brighton and Seaford or Eastbourne.*

This page, top - *The up and down main platforms temporarily out of use. The view is looking towards the tunnel and the London direction.*

This page, middle and bottom - *Some of the wooden boarding removed to release the flood water from the adjacent cattle market.*
The Lens of Sutton Association (1).

NOVEMBER 1960: LEWES - AWASH

From the 'RAILWAY MAGAZINE'. 1/1961.

"Twenty different locomotives took part in the operation of steam substitute trains around Lewes over three days in November, when after continuous heavy rain, tracks in the station there were flooded and no electric services could be run. Mr. R. A. H. Weight writes that the classes represented were West Country No. 34098; 'K', 'Ul' and 'N' 2-6-0; 'C' and 'Q' '0-6-0', 'M7' 0-4-4 tank ; and standard class '4' 4-6-0 and (numerically the largest) 2-6-4 tank. Steam trains, with a variety of locomotives and rolling stock, and some made up to eight or nine modern coaches, ran spasmodically between Brighton and Eastbourne at first, on Friday, November 4. However, lighter trains on the following day provided as far as possible a half-hourly service, though taking longer than the quickly-accelerating multiple-unit sets normally do. Steam services were continued for a time on Sunday, November 6. Brighton-Uckfield trains could not be run during this period, because of other flooding, which was even more severe on the Keymer Junction-London side of Lewes Station, and beyond the tunnel, necessitating lengthier complete closure. Hastings-Eastbourne-Victoria electric trains, when able to be run, travelled by way of Brighton (reverse) and the main line *via* Hassocks. Two six-car diesel-electric sets from the London-Hastings, *via* Tunbridge Wells, service also took part in the emergency Eastbourne-Brighton operations, with St. Leonards drivers, and were able to keep more closely to normal timings. A steam push-and-pull train, with an 'M7' locomotive, provided the Lewes-Seaford branch connections in spells. To speed connections from the Brighton direction, a number of the electric trains usually running through half-hourly, but temporarily restricted to the Ore-Hastings-Eastbourne stretch, making use of the triangular junctions ran *via* Polegate eastbound and took up passengers there from the special steam trains to avoid their having to travel into Eastbourne (or Hampden Park) and out again."

"Mr. Weight adds that, as for a time certain bus services were also cut or diverted in the district, numerous passengers were rightly appreciative of the revised rail services quickly arranged under difficult circumstances."

One of the LMR 2-6-4T engines drafted on to the Southern shortly after nationalisation to fulfil an urgent need for a large tank engine. (The BR 80xxx series would later take over these duties.) The train is a Brighton to Victoria service, running via East Grinstead and Oxted.

R C Riley / The Transport Treasury

In 1947 my parents and I moved to a new house on the Landport Estate where, between the houses, I could observe the London line on the downgrade into Lewes. Here I could see the regular hourly electrics on the London expresses, which if I recall correctly, were usually a 6-PUL / 6-PAN combination with the occasional substitution of various 4-Cor combinations to make up a twelve car formation. Local services to Haywards Heath and on to Horsted Keynes were handled by 2-BIL sets.

Early days at the Pells Infants School would take me on a footbridge over the line near to the entrance to Lewes tunnel and where trains would often be stopped at the signals. On seeing the train stop, we children would run to the bridge where, on some occasions, the train would be emitting a rather nose-tingling smell. I have been told since that the smell was ozone: why don't EMUs give off this smell these days?

The Newhaven Boat trains also passed Landport, and, in the summer, often two or three relief boat trains as well, The main train would usually be 'Hornby' hauled, but the reliefs would have steam haulage: Bullied Pacifics, 'King Arthurs', 'Schools', Atlantics, and I seem to recall the occasional 'Nelson'. The variety of coaching stock and liveries was always of interest, and not always of Southern origin too. One peculiarity I remember from those days, and only had confirmed in recent times, was green-liveried Pullman cars in the Boat trains. It was only when I read that at that time B.R were short of Dining cars and bought some surplus Pullman cars from the Pullman Company that I could confirm my memory wasn't playing tricks with me. *(Several of these were indeed former Hastings line Pullman vehicles – Ed.)*

Another peculiar memory from around those years, was

Lewes, 11 July 1958. The scene is from the main Brighton platforms with the divergence of the Uckfield (left) and route to Southerham Junction (right). Lewes Junction signal box is visible. The location of the turntable was beyond and opposite the signal box in the 'V' of the junction of the two routes.

The Lens of Sutton Association.

USA tank DS237, the former No. 30065, in the process of transfer from Eastleigh to Ashford, 8 December 1963. Mark Abbott accompanied the engine throughout, recording various scenes en-route including an overnight stop at Brighton. Not surprisingly the limited speed possible, allied to a tendency for the type to run-hot if run too fast meant that the journey was somewhat laborious with numerous enforced lay-bys en route to allow other trains to pass. *Mark Abbott*

a five-car Brighton Belle electric set passing through Lewes on a Sunday. Again I would discover later this was a regular summer turn on a special 'extra' to Eastbourne.

Of a morning I would be awoken by the passing of the newspaper train rushing down the bank towards Lewes. This was usually an 0-4-4 tank engine and two vans, I would imagine an 'H' class from Three Bridges Depot. At night I could lie in bed and listen to a heavy freight train climbing out of Lewes. Whilst the bank isn't particularly steep, it is a steady climb for some distance, and the steam loco could be heard fighting its way upwards with the sound heard for many minutes over several miles.

The railway and the Ouse are in close proximity on the run down into Lewes especially in the vicinity of Landport. Most winters the adjacent fields flood to some degree, but the worst was in 1960 with much of the town also engulfed. Shortly before Lewes tunnel, the lower part of the bank was covered to quite a depth, as was much of Lewes station. Consequently the power to the third rail had to be switched off. No trains could enter Lewes from the London line with the Brighton lines platforms affected as well. In the London platforms, water was up to platform level, whilst on the cattle market side of these platforms, the south west

side, the platforms and the wooden platform shelter boardings was acting like a dam to waters which were building up and already flooding houses in that vicinity. The local council approached British Railways with a proposal to blow up the platform and so release the water. B.R. refused, but did agree to remove some of the boarding: as seen in one of the photographs, which did relieve the situation to some extent. The railway then arranged for two large pumps to be brought on well wagons from Peterborough to ease the problem further.

Meanwhile although the flooding in the Brighton platforms had eased somewhat, it still was not possible to restore the current to the third rail, the London lines and the track on the London side of Lewes tunnel being still under quite a depth of water. Brighton steam shed however, came to the rescue, and having mustered as many loco-hauled coaches as they could, ran a skeleton service from Brighton via Lewes to Eastbourne and Seaford – it is one of these services that can be seen in another accompanying photograph. It was five days before the waters receded enough for a near normal electric service to be resumed. Incidentally, overlooking the Brighton line platforms and on the opposite side of the roadway above, was a water softening tower

43

and a large water storage tank serving the railway water columns. These were removed some years after the end of steam, although the brick base of the tank remains.

To return to Lewes station in drier and happier times, the Uckfield line curved away to the north from the junction. Most of the trains, all steam of course before diesels took over in the mid-60s, were either for East Grinstead (until closure) or Tunbridge Wells and Tonbridge. However a number of trains were through trains to or from London via Oxted. It was not unknown for these latter trains, often of six or more coaches and often with Bulleid Pacifics at the head, to stall on this curving incline. The solution to the problem, was, under the watchful eye of the signalman at the busy main box, Lewes Junction, to reverse into the station and try again. Apparently it was also not unknown for an electric train to be inadvertently misrouted onto this line. If it came to rest beyond the reach of the third rail, a steam locomotive was sent out to haul the set back before it could be correctly routed away.

An ex-signalman at Lewes told me of an amusing tale involving a rather portly relief signalman at Lewes Junction box many years ago. Apparently he was having trouble operating a ground signal for a train movement. Much straining and swearing ensued until, in utter frustration he shouted to the signal lad who was returning to the box from the station, to give the offending ground signal a kick to see if that would do the trick. The lad did as he was asked but to no avail. The signalman cursed some more and was on the point of requesting assistance from the signal engineers when the signal lad walked into the box, went over to the lever, put his foot on the treadle and released the lever. Due to his rather large frontage, the relief signalman had not seen the treadle.

In the 'V' formed between the Uckfield and Eastbourne lines, there had once been a turntable used by the engines of steam services terminating at Lewes. It was removed long before my appearance on the scene in 1943, but the turntable well remains to this day, at one time made into a beautiful flowerbed but now sadly neglected.

Whilst talking to people about memories of the railway

Left - Having been displaced elsewhere, the 4-COR sets ended their days on local duties. An unidentified set in corporate blue livery passing an almost full set of exchange sidings.
Right - The water softening and storage tank at the station now redundant and in the process of removal.

Looking towards the London line and Tunnel. This is the avoiding line that curved round beside Pinwell lane to, firstly, Lewes goods yard and then the marshalling yard before rejoining the main line about half a mile north of Southerham Junction. In the vicinity of the goods yard, the avoiding line passed underneath the Uckfield line by means of a bridge.

The Lens of Sutton Association.

The former Lewes Goods Yard signal box, (previously Lewes East but renamed and downgraded to a non-block post from March 1889) and which was finally taken out of use in November 1966. It is seen here with the nearby marshalling yard now devoid of traffic in the process of being removed. The view is towards Southerham Junction. The goods and various other private sidings were behind the photographer.

at Lewes, I discovered an interesting little snippet. Apparently close to the station, near to Pinwell Lane: which runs beside what were the tracks to the goods and marshalling yard, were gardens owned by the railway and worked by two railway employees. From here plants were grown for distribution to stations on the Southern and intended for use in the requisite station gardens. Pinwell Lane still exists, as does the area of the old marshalling yard, the latter now partially excavated - probably to remove contaminated soil, and has been turned into a wetland park. At the entrance is an old level crossing gate as a reminder of its former use. Following one of the paths within the park will lead to the main Eastbourne and Seaford line, also a small cabin painted in Southern colours. This had once been a ground frame at Uckfield station and is now being used as a bird hide at the new location.

From the same spot, by turning around with your back to the railway and looking towards the cliffs, is where the old ce-ment works was sited. Just to the right where the river curves, is the remains of the wharf and slightly beyond that, where the works branch crossed the road. Following the main line now, just across the river bridge and below the new road bridge is Southerham Junction, nowadays slightly re-located, and the site of the exchange sidings. Where the right hand upright of the bridge now stands once stood the junction signal box from where the signalman used to be in contact with the foreman at the adjacent chalkpit. This communication was necessary as once or twice a day chalk blasting would take place. The foreman would thus contact the signalman for permission to carry out the blasting, and, if no trains were due, the all clear would be given by the signalman displaying a white flag.

I would like to thank Ian and Jim Colwell, both ex- B.R. signalmen and Bob Spooner, ex-B.R. driver, for their help in compiling this article.

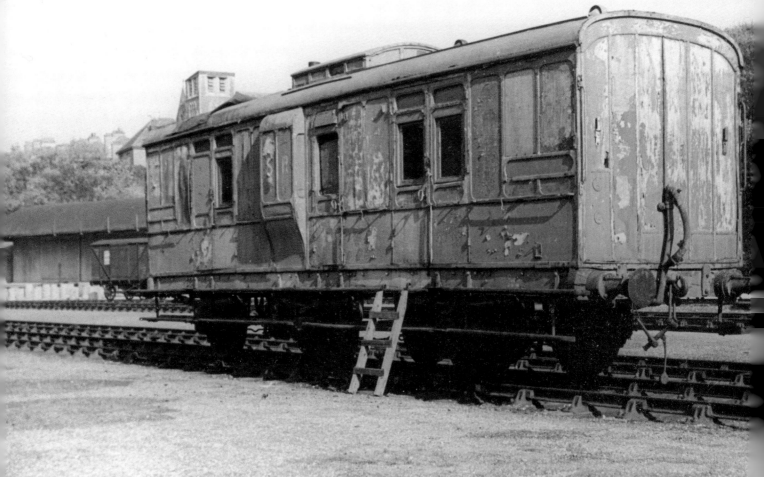

Terry Cole's Rolling Stock File No. 12

'Retired' Vehicles

The Southern was always very careful not to discard anything which could be put to further use. In this 'File' we look at three vehicles finding useful employment after their 'traffic' days are over.

Opposite top - Camping Coach Holidays were very popular from the mid-thirties through to the sixties and provided families with the opportunity for a cheap holiday in the country. Many wayside stations would feature one or more vehicles in a quiet corner. For the railway company it was a good means of getting income out of otherwise life-expired coaches. This delightful picture, taken at Newton Poppleford on 2 July 1952, shows SR camping coaches Nos. S3 and S11. No. S3 was an ex London Chatham and Dover Railway 28ft five-compartment 3rd built in January 896 as LCD No.153. It became SECR No. 3107 then SR No. 1675 before being converted to a Camping Coach in 1935. No. S11 was a similar vehicle built March 1897 as LCD No. 1218. It became SECR No. 3420 then SR No. 1764 and it too was converted in 1935. Both vehicles were scrapped in 1953.

Opposite bottom - Many railway companies were fond of building separate four or six-wheel guards and luggage vans for use on their passenger trains, and many expresses in the first two decades of the twentieth century would include one or more such vehicles in their formation. No. 1282s, seen here finishing its days as a mobile store at Kemp Town Brighton, was one of 79 centre birdcage six- wheeled guards vans built by the SECR between 1902 and 1906. They were built on a wooden underframe and were 36ft long, 8ft 4 in wide over duckets and 12ft 9in high over the birdcage roof. The SR allocated Diagram No 885. Their use on passenger trains came to an end in the 1930s and those surviving after Nationalisation did so in departmental use. An example still exists on the Bluebell Railway where it is awaiting restoration.

Below - This freshly painted van, No. S42978, was one of a large number of a large number of similar unfitted 10 ton goods vans built from about 1913 onwards for the London and South Western Railway. Seen here on 30 August 1951 at Newhaven Harbour, its branding shows it has been relegated to Internal Use only within the docks. Unusually it has been given a full repaint including its running number.   [All photos author's collection]

FROM SALISBURY TO DORSET
- via Downton and Fordingbridge

The recent publication by Nigel Bray on the Salisbury & Dorset Junction Railway*, prompted a search amongst out own archive of material and a few questions to our own contacts to see if there might be anything more available - apologies also, the intended slot in Issue 11 for this piece just did not occur!

The results are seen over the next few pages. Further coverage then, on a line previously mostly ignored by historians but now at last given a definite treatment by Nigel. (We know of the existence of other staff views from the route which Alan Postlethwaite will be including in a piece on 'Southern railwaymen' due to appear in a future issue of 'SW'.)

* Kestrel Railway Books.

The northern extremity of the route and its junction with the Romsey - Salisbury line at Alderbury Junction. The former double junction was altered to that seen, a facing crossover and single lead on the branch from 27 June 1943, the revised arrangement considered cheaper on maintenance with the abolition of the former diamond crossing. The signal box dated from 1889 and replaced an earlier structure, presumably on the same site. It remained in use until 1970, six years after the branch was closed, and contained a frame of just 14 levers. The trespass notice was a warning to any persons using what was a staff platform - located immediately behind the photographer. It ceased to be used from the same time as the branch closed, 4 May 1964.

Lens of Sutton

Downton station depicted here in the rain on 27 July 1957. The location was a stopping place mid-section between Alderbury Junction and Breamore, the loop having been converted to a siding and the signal box reclassified as a ground frame from 1 December 1922. Clearly the LSWR were intent on economy nearly 80 years ago. Seen is the 10.27 a.m. Salisbury to Bournemouth West service arriving behind T9 No. 30707.

J H Aston

Above - No 76017 (- the one that fell down the bank at Whitchurch in 1954) heading north through Downton on 27 July 1957 with the regular 8.48am New Milton to Swansea through service. **Bottom right** - Four years later, sister engine, No 76005 arrives at Fordingbridge with the 5.20pm from Salisbury. **Bottom left and centre left** - Not long before the line closed, Mark Abbott made a footplate trip on the line this time on No. 76029. He recorded several views on the way one of which was this cab view showing the Breamore to Alderbury Junction tablet in its pouch

This page, top - Fordingbridge was without doubt the largest and most important station on the 18¼ mile route. No footbridge was provided and instead passengers were encouraged to make use of the pathways leading up to the roadbridge at the north end of the station - probably many used the board crossing instead.

This page, centre - An unidentified 'Mogul' arriving with a mixes three coach set bound for Salisbury. Seen from the vantage point of the aforementioned road bridge, the curvature associated with the line at this point is apparent, with 66 chain and 80 chain radius curves immediately behind the train.

This page, bottom - North through the platforms and the pathway from the platform to the road bridge can be discerned. Whilst level through the platform there was a short climb at 1 in 105 immediately upon leaving, certainly not the steepest part of the route, this being a section at 1 in 75 north of Downton accompanied by a 38 chain radius curve. Indeed the whole route was very much a switchback and tortuous line.

Opposite top - Views of goods yards are always welcome, this showing three of the five sidings in the yard at Fordingbridge, probably not long before closure.

Opposite bottom - The exterior of the 12 lever LSWR 1875 signal box. Originally of 11 levers the frame was extended by 1912. In addition, it was reported there was a further 2-lever open air lever frame, the purpose of which is not recorded. No doubt originally of standard LSWR timber braced construction, the front panels are seen here with asbestos cladding.

Above - Waterloo. *A train of empty Maunsell stock from Bricklayers Arms approaches Hungerford bridge. Rebuilt light Pacific No. 34005 Barnstaple runs tender-first in order to head a subsequent train from Charing Cross to the Kent coast. The picture is taken from the footbridge linking the SER and L&SWR stations, built above the former junction platform. Tall surrounding buildings include the Union Jack Club (left) and the Shell Building (under construction).*

Opposite top - London Bridge. *The London & Greenwich Railway opened in 1836. Its London end was used by the SER who absorbed the L&G in 1845. The north side of London Bridge became a through station in 1864 when the SER opened its extensions to Cannon Street and Charing Cross. Almost a century later, the platform canopies still have SER valancing. The art deco lamp post is late SR. Light Pacific No. 34021 Dartmoor trundles through a deserted platform 3 with a mid-morning train to the Channel ports. In 1958, London Bridge had 21 platforms.*

Opposite bottom - London Bridge Low-level. *Here was the terminus of the London & Greenwich Railway. The London & Croydon terminus was originally to its north, later rebuilt as the SER through station. Wedged between the latter and the large LB&SCR terminus to the south, this backwater became known as London Bridge Low-level. In 1959, it comprised four terminal platforms which were used for parcels and for peak-hour EMU services to Tattenham Corner and Caterham. This parcels train is headed by class D1 4-4-0 No. 31739.*

THE SOUTH EASTERN MAIN LINE

Final Wisps of Steam

Alan Postlethwaite

This excursion follows the SER main line from London to Dover. It records trains and infrastructure between 1958 and 1961 when Kentish steam came to an end. Historical facts and figures are drawn from C.F. Dendy Marshall's *History of the Southern Railway*, revised by R.W. Kidner and published by Ian Allan in 1963. The pictures are the author's.

Above - Redhill. *The original 1842 SER main line from London Bridge used other companies' metals as far as Redhill before turning east on to its own line to Dover. The SER line to Reading opened in 1849. After the Sevenoaks cut-off opened, Redhill became a reversing station for services between the GWR and the south coast, for heavy freight to and from the GWR and L&SWR, and for military traffic. A class N Mogul is seen backing on to a Reading train in the Up loop platform. The signal posts have SR mechanical route indicators for Tonbridge, Brighton and Guildford.*

*Opposite bottom - **Dunton Green**. In order to compete effectively with the LC&DR's more direct route to Dover, the SER built its main line 'cut-off' via Sevenoaks to Tonbridge which opened in 1868. Coasting down from Polhill tunnel, 'Schools' class No. 30922 'Marlborough' heads a long parcels train from either London Bridge or Bricklayers Arms. Until dieselisation in 1958, the 'Schools' were the mainstay of Hastings passenger services. During WW2, this engine was shot up by the Luftwaffe around Westenhanger.*

***Above - Sevenoaks**. The London end of Sevenoaks station was crossed at a skew by the A21 road bridge and had a spectacular array of SR signal brackets which served all five Up platform faces. The SR running-in board has had 'Tubs Hill' painted out, an old suffix to differentiate it from the nearby 'Bat and Ball' station of the LC&DR. Trains from the latter generally terminated in the foreground road where class H tank No. 31505 is standing: this platform was also signalled for reversible working. Harry Wainwright's 'pagoda' roof on No. 31505 is distinctive. The wagons are carrying materials for Weald tunnel electrification work. Lines from Sevenoaks were electrified to London in 1935 and to Tonbridge in 1961. **Bottom - Dunton Green**. The Westerham branch opened in 1881. For reasons unknown, a long mixed freight, bound for the Channel ports, takes refuge here on the initial curve of the branch, headed by class N Mogul No. 31828. Dunton Green's station buildings are visible in the background and the home signal is leaning several degrees out of true. The train presently reversed on to the Up Main before crossing back onto the Down line.*

Top - Weald Tunnel. A Hastings DEMU bursts forth from the south portal of Weald tunnel into the rich countryside of the low Weald. It passes an Up express to Victoria headed by light Pacific No. 34070 Manston. The SR signal bracket has an exceptionally long platform for visibility from within the tunnel. A colour light repeater distant signal at the other (north) end of the tunnel was unique to the SR.
Bottom - Weald Intermediate. Wild flowers and grasses enhance this wooden signal box built in SER vernacular style. It is served by two sets of telegraph poles connected by an overhead cable. Passing at speed is light Pacific No. 34078 222 Squadron with a train to Charing Cross. It commemorates the Spitfire pilots from Linconshire who scored 49 victories during the Battle of Britain in the skies hereabouts.

Tonbridge. *Starter signals of the Up island platform were mounted on a massive lattice gantry dating from the 1935 remodelling of the junction. This long, tapered cantilever frames a local train coming off the old SER main line from Redhill. It is headed by standard class 4 tank No. 80147. The ball factory on the right is a reminder that cricket originated in this neck of the woods.*

Above - Tonbridge. *Grotesque shadows of a water column play upon the tender of class N Mogul No. 31826 as it prepares to depart the Down platform. The leading coach is an SE&CR ten-compartment third. Looming above is the massive bridge of the booking office and A21 trunk road. Four single-track arches span the lines, forming a symbolic gateway to the Garden of England. The Hastings line comes in from the right where two railwaymen are crossing the Up tracks.*

Paddock Wood. *This Bank Holiday excursion of immaculate Bulleid stock is headed by light Pacific No. 34092 City of Wells. Having just shed its pilot (Schools class 4-4-0 No. 30932 Blundells), it is restarting for the Maidstone West line beneath an SR signal gantry. Meanwhile, a fast train is signalled along the main line to infinity. The ancient SER overhead signal box spans the start of the Hawkhurst branch which parallels the main line for half a mile. The trailing 3-way point to the Up platform was characteristic of many SE&CR stations.*

***Top - Near Paddock Wood**. Engineered by William Cubitt, the South Eastern main line along the low Weald was almost dead straight and easily graded at no greater than 1 in 264. This compares with 1 in 120 on the Sevenoaks cut-off, 1 in 97 on the Hastings line and 1 in 60 just south of Maidstone West. Bound for Maidstone West, 0-4-4 class H tank No. 31553 heads a smart set of BR Mark Ones which are fifty years younger than the locomotive. The ballast bin and huts are neat products from Exmouth Junction's precast concrete works. **Bottom - Ashford**. The London end of Ashford was approached beneath a road bridge of single-track arches similar to those at Tonbridge. Blowing steam and shunting vans is 2-6-4 standard class 4 tank No. 80040. Parcels are piled on the Down platform. The arc roof canopy and brick chimneys are part of the original single storey building which was surprisingly modest for this important junction station. The flatter canopy on the right with plain slotted valancing is part of an SE&CR make-over. The station these days has a quite different look as Ashford International.*

Ashford. *Blowing cylinders and making a fine column of steam in 1958, class L No. 31781 heads a train of Bulleid stock bound for Canterbury West and Margate. This was Harry Wainwright's heaviest class of 4-4-0, introduced in 1914 following an easement of weight restrictions. No. 781 was the last of a batch built in Berlin by Borsig, assembled and proven at Ashford by a German workforce and completed on the opening day of the First World War. The canopy style is SE&CR.*

Top - Near Ashford. Class D was Wainwright's first 4-4-0 express engine of which 51 were built between 1901 and 1903. No. 489 was from the final batch of ten, built for the SE&CR by Dubs & Co. From 1921, many were rebuilt by Maunsell as class D1. Just one is preserved - No. 737 which can be seen these days in SE&CR livery at the NRM, York.

Bottom - Smeeth. This station opened in 1851 and closed to passengers in 1954. By 1961, it had been converted into a private bungalow. The 'ghosts of passengers past' wait on the Up platform as an express thunders through, headed by light Pacific No. 31083 605 Squadron. With four vans, this train may have been one half of a two-part boat train. The engine commemorates the Hurricane pilots from Scotland who achieved 56 victories during the Battle of Britain.

Opposite top - Near Smeeth. *The prototype class U1 Mogul was a rebuild of the only 3-cylinder version of class K tank - No. 890 River Frome. No. 31908 was from a batch of twenty built at Eastleigh in 1931. Very clean and making a crisp plume of exhaust steam, it heads a Continental fitted freight which includes two wagon-loads of motor-cars.*

Opposite bottom - Near Smeeth. *The 'Golden Arrow' was the SR's most prestigious boat train. It was a brilliant PR initiative of Sir John Elliot who became General Manager of the SR and then Chairman of the Railway Executive and of London Transport. Of the 110 light Pacifics built by the Southern, sixty were rebuilt by BR, losing their air-smoothed casing in the process. No. 34100 Appledore looks immaculate as it heads the Up 'Golden Arrow' in 1961.*

Above - Dover. *The SER reached Dover in 1844, followed by the LC&DR in 1861. There was fierce competition for Continental traffic until the pooling of revenues was agreed in 1865. The SE&CR merger in 1899 was followed by rationalisation and the opening of Dover Marine station in 1914. In 1959, three heavy Pacifics were allocated to Stewarts Lane MPD for Dover boat train duties - Channel Packet, Clan Line and Rotterdam Lloyd. In rebuilt form, No. 35015 Rotterdam Lloyd gathers speed out of Dover on the approach to Shakespeare tunnel. It is hauling the Up 'Golden Arrow' of Pullman stock plus a few ordinary coaches and luggage vans. To achieve short journey times, heavy luggage was originally inspected by Customs officers in absentia and delivered to passengers' addresses in London or Paris. Those were the days!*

'REBUILT'-THE LETTERS AND COMMENTS PAGE(S)

We are due a definite catch-up in our Letters and Comments pages, thus in no particular order (other than mostly in Issue sequence), here we go:

The collapse of the signal Clapham Junction, Issue 7, continues to arouse interest. This from Colin Hall, "In 1965 I was a regular commuter on the Guildford via Effingham Junction to Waterloo service: the '42'. On that Monday, like most other days, I passed through Clapham Junction before 8.30 a.m. - I had to be in Bloomsbury for 9.00 a.m. The news that Waterloo was closed filtered through to me during the day and I chose to make my way home from Canon Street - a station I had never used before or since. On the station concourse I remember that I was picked on by a plain clothes policeman, 'Could I help with an ID parade?' Of all the days to choose, I explained my dilemma and politely declined. I eventually reached Effingham Junction via Epson, although 44 years on I cannot recall anything about the journey, except that I reached home in East Horsley by walking back through the local woods and it was still daylight."

In Issue 8 we were proud to include the brief history of Woking Homes. Since that time much in the way of snippets have arrived adding much to the obvious gaps in the original article. This then from Mr.N S Barney of Poole:

"I should first explain my involvement with 'The Orphanage' (as it was always known in Woking). I was born in Woking and lived within a mile of the Orphanage from the time of WW2 until 1984. My father had been a resident from the death of his father in 1925 (my grandfather had been a shunter at Andover Junction) until he reached school leaving age in the 1930s. My earliest recollections of the establishment was when I accompanied my parents to the Old Boys and Girls Association Reunions held at the Orphanage. These reunions were held annually on the third Saturday in October. We also made other visits, as my father was, at that time, involved with the running of the scout troop and also to see various members of staff, some of whom had been there whilst my father was an inmate. This eventually lead to my own involvement with the model and miniature railways. I am able therefore to add something to the information published.

"In the caption to the view of the general office, on Page 31, it refers to Mr Wells, (Tommy), as being the Secretary Superintendent, his position was actually that of the Office Manager, dealing with the administration side of the organisation. The Secretary Superintendent at this time was the well-respected Mr A G Evershed, as in the photo on Page 30. Indeed, he was by far and away the longest serving person in this post, his term of office stretching from some time in the 1930s through to the 1970s. The initials A G stood for Alldred George, although he preferred to be known as George. Latterly he also served as a JP on the Woking bench. During most of this time, the Chairman of the governors was Mr Fred Price, a Running Foreman at Guildford shed.

"On Page 29 when referring to the mosaic tiling and the headstone, it rightly states that they did not survive the demolition, this is true, however the heavy wooden entrance doors with glass panels depicting a stylised LSWR locomotive, together with the two matching side screens again with engraved /etched railway screens were incorporated into the new building, although sadly not in a very prominent position.

"The caption on Page 24 refers to the possibility of there being a live-steam line around the grounds. I can confirm there was, as from 1963 until 1984 I was very much involved in its operation. A brief history of the railway may be of interest to readers.

"The railway was started by a gentleman by the name of Frederick R Huchinson in the early years of the 20th century. For many years prior to, and immediately after WW2, Mr Hutchinson operated a portable 6" gauge line - during several summer months prior to the war this line was set up on Hove Lawns. The proceeds from these operations were donated to the orphanage. Incidentally Mr Hutchinson was the father of W.J. (Joe) Hutchinson, a senior draughtsman at Brighton, as referred to on Page 79 of SW No 1.

"Moving on to how the railway came to Woking, we must go back to the O gauge layout. During a visit to the Orphanage two young railway employees, Alan Brown of BR's Headquarters staff and Max Millard of the Southern Region's CM&EE's department (also mentioned on page 79 of SW No 1), found the layout almost derelict and asked if they could renovate it. This was agreed and they set about the task. On hearing of Mr F Hutchinson's death and as the operation of the miniature railway was not going to be continued by his family, a request was made if it could come to Woking at least on loan, to continue fund raising, This was agreed to and most of the railway, consisting of the portable track, two of the locomotives and the rolling stock came to Woking. The fund raising continued by taking the portable track to various events within easy travelling distance. Just prior to my involvement at the end of 1963, the ground level line around the football pitch, on what was known as the Boys Field, was begun. This ground level line was built using wooden sleepers, properly ballasted with granite chippings, supporting flat bottom aluminium rail, eventually extended all the way round the field. In its final form it included a station, tunnel and turntable, together with workshop and storage facilities. Subsequent to the sale of the original Orphanage and field for redevelopment, a new line was built around the new home. This new line was of dual 6" and 7¼" gauge, but I understand has now been abandoned. (2009).

"The following is a brief description of the locomotives and rolling stock, The design of the earliest locomotive was based on a Drummond T14 'Paddle box' 4-6-0, to the now obsolete track gauge of 6", although there is reason to believe that it may have been started as 5" gauge. Some time later this locomotive was modified to resemble a Urie HI5. The next locomotive, built in 1925, was a 4-6-2 with a bogie tender large enough for the driver to ride in. As built, this locomotive reflected characteristics of a 'Gresley Pacific', akin also to the Greenly Pacifies for the RHDR, with the cylinders and valve gear based on those of a 'King Arthur'. Over the years Mr Hutchinson carried out various modifications, the final one an overall casing in attempt to replicate a Bulleid Pacific. It was in this form that it arrived at Woking. Subsequent modifications were carried out by us, including removal of the casing and trying to make it appear in outline at least, as that of the projected Maunsell Pacific that was never built. It carried the number 870, as it was felt that could well have been the identification allocated had the Maunsell locomotives been built. Subsequently, Mr Hutchinson built a model of Lord Nelson, although unfortunately this never came to Woking. The rolling stock consisted of three very long 4-wheel coaches, each capable accommodating four adults seated face to face in two pairs. Whilst the long wheel base was perfectly satisfactory when running on a straight portable track, this arrangement was unsuitable for the ground level line which contained curves. These three coaches where therefore modified into a 3-car articulated set. This was achieved by building two new bogies, for the outer ends plus two centre bogies utilising four of the original wheel sets. The two remaining wheel sets were eventually used under a battery electric locomotive. Subsequently an extra three car set, again articulated, was built at Woking.

			BRITISH RAILWAYS
			SOUTHERN REGION

5344

Department .... MOTIVE POWER

Name HARRIS E.W.V.

Grade DRIVER

Station FOLKESTONE JUNCTION

Standard Deductions - Year 1956

I give below details of the standard weekly amount to be deducted from your wages/salary commencing with the first week of the year.

PARTICULARS	FUND No.	£	AMOUNT s.	d.
S.R. (SOUTHAMPTON SPORTS & SOCIAL CLUB)	2			
HOUSING LOAN	3			
RAILWAY BENEVOLENT INSTITUTION	5		2	0
S.R. CLERICAL STAFF PROVIDENT DEATH FUND	6			
S.R. SALARIED STAFF ASSISTANCE FUND	7			
B.R. (S.R.) LOCO. DEPT. DEATH, INJURY & PROV. SOCTY.	8			
S.R. ENGINEMEN & FIREMEN'S MUTUAL ASSURANCE	9			4
S.R. (WESTERN SECTION) PROVIDENT SOCIETY	11			
S.E. & C. SICK & BENEFIT SOCIETY	12			
S.R. ENGINEMEN, FIREMEN, CLEANERS, ETC., SICK SOCIETY	13			
B.R. (S.R.) SUPPLEMENTARY PENSION SOCIETY	14			
S.R. (S.E. & C.) ENGINEMEN & MOTORMEN PENSION FUND SOCIETY	15		2	3
L. & S.W. ENGINE DRIVERS, FIREMEN ETC., PENSION SOCIETY	16			
L.B. & S.C. PENSION FUND	17			
SUPERANNUATION FUND	18			
PROVIDENT MUTUAL LIFE ASSURANCE	19			
SAVINGS BANK	20			
HOUSE RENT	21			
S.R. ORPHANAGE	22			4
RAILWAY CONVALESCENT HOMES	23			3
HOSPITAL SAVING ASSOCIATION	24			6
SEASON TICKET (AFTER _____ WEEKS)	25			
SPORTS CLUB	26			
INSTITUTE	27-29			
TOOLS FOR APPRENTICES	31			
B.R. (S.R.) BRUNSWICK HOUSE INSTITUTE & CLUB	32			
B.R. (S.R.) STAFF ASSOCIATION	33			4
WAGES GRADES PENSION SCHEME	34		3	4
NATIONAL INSURANCE	35		6	9
TOTAL STANDARD DEDUCTION		£	14	4

16·7

Kindly submitted by Jeremy O'Keeffe as an example of the 4d weekly deduction to the SR Orphanage paid by his Grandfather.

"As an aside to railway matters, at the time the picture of the naval gun on Page 26 was taken, the Sea Cadet Headquarters was at the junction of Brewery Road and Chobham Road, on a piece of land between Brewery Road and the Basingstoke Canal. When this site was redeveloped, if my memory serves me correctly the Sea Cadets and gun relocated to Kingfield near Woking Football Clubs ground, near to but not in the actual park."

Alan Blackburn adds much interesting, and I will freely admit, amusing comment to various aspects of Issue 9. "I've said it before, but each issue of 'SW' stirs old memories........Kent Coast Electrification. The Down Night Ferry one evening in the Autumn of 1959. The train had the usual formation with a normal BR coach next the engine for the 'foot passengers' - who were usually young railwaymen going over to Europe for their annual fix of what a railway should be i.e. the SBB. Without this we would all have lost heart in the industry long ago and joined our mates at Heathrow.

"All went well until somewhere beyond Faversham when the pantograph on the E5000 went up, presumably all of its own accord, and was promptly wrecked by the next overbridge. The driver coasted to Selling and there, not unreasonably, declared the engine a failure.

"Assistance was, we were told, on its way from Dover, but in the meantime it was decided that the failed engine should be uncoupled. Now this was going to be good entertainment because the only person who could do this filthy job was the Guard and our Guard was the Guard of the Night Ferry, complete with a superior overcoat, flower in the button-hole *and* immaculate shoes!

"Now Passenger Guards were not by this time, the most highly respected of railwaymen amongst their peers ,whilst we as Signalmen regarded ourselves as the elite! I do remember that we restrained ourselves from any direct comment, beyond offering to hold his overcoat and mentioning how dirty such a job was, but to watch the poor man struggling with the coupling and brake pipes, whilst trying to keep clean was a sight I can remember as if it was last night!

"Poisonous Porton. The military lands around Porton are very extensive and border the West of England main line for some miles. Thus it was that one day in the 1980s at the height or the IRA troubles, the p-way Patrolman is walking his length near Porton, when down comes a helicopter and out jump a group of armed soldiers who seize the poor chap and fly off with him. One imagines that he was not very happy. His Inspector at Andover was similarly not happy, nor was the Divisional Engineer at Wimbledon, who wanted the matter raised with the MoD. The Chief Civil Engineer did indeed write to the General Manager, but by this time those concerned were rather amused by the whole affair and the poor man was Irish after all. There are not many Irish p-way men in that part of the world.

"The photograph of the lorry shown loading a 'Demountable-flat' on Page 4 was indeed taken at Nine Elms. These flats were introduced by the London & South Western to improve the turn-round time of the lorries operating there. The idea was that the flat would stand on the old horse cart being loaded and then when this was completed, which could take some time, it would be transshipped on to the next available lorry, thus saving it having to stand idle whilst it was loaded. It was called increased productivity, there is little new in the world! Incidentally I once worked with a Signalman whose father was a farrier at Nine Elms Goods. He and another Farrier had over a hundred horses each to look after, both road delivery and shunting horses which were used on the river wharf.

"The 'C' class No. 31054 was not the only one of these engines at Feltham in the autumn of 1959. I witnessed two young drivers each 'armed' with a 'C' having a 'pushing match' one against the other, one morning at the West end of Feltham Yard. A lot of noise and slipping but no clear winner. The driver of the 'up hump' 350hp who was with me, observed that they were Brighton engines and 'not much use' - having mistaken their Stirling steam reversers for Westinghouse pumps! What they were sent to Feltham to do I cannot imagine. I was a signalman at Feltham East at the time and never saw one on a train. They could usefully have replaced the M7s on the station shunt, but I do not think they ever did that." (Gerry Bixley, amongst others, has provided even more information on the 'Demountable-flat'. Again this will feature in more detail, hopefully in Issue 13- ED.)

From John Snell, reference Issue No. 10. "The photo of the 'M7' at Launceston in 1944. This is rare and would have been the Bude based 'M7' which worked a Sunday only train: Bude to Launceston in the 1940s. Most North Cornwall trains were hauled by tender engines like the Maunsell 'N' or Drummond 'T9' types."

Also re Issue No. 10 from Mr. D G Brown of Orpington, " The photograph on page 83 is the first I have ever seen published of what is probably one of the least photogenic locations on the Southern. It is, however, quite historic in that Holborn Viaduct and Blackfriars were equipped with the first four-aspect signals installed in this country in 1926, shortly to be followed by lines to Charing Cross and Cannon Street.

"Holborn Viaduct was a six platform station, but only three were used after electrification, Nos. 1, 4 & 5 were extended to cope with 8 cars. The other three platforms were only of about 4 car length and were used for newspaper and parcels traffic. [The arches could not be widened further since the lines led into the bridge over Ludgate Hill which could not be made steeper as the State Coach used by the Monarch on ceremonial occasions had no brakes and its speed could thus only be controlled by the horses - it still has no brakes today!] In addition to the electric trains terminating at Holborn Viaduct, there were empty stock workings between Cannon Street and Stewarts Lane running round at the derelict Ludgate Hill station before the evening peak and after the morning peak. It is one of these movements that No. 31102 is involved in. From memory, I believe there were 4 or 5 trains involved in the these movements both morning and evening.

"Lastly there were conditional timings to and from the widened lines, most for Hither Green sidings, but a few to or from Herne Hill sorting sidings and Wandsworth Road. The timings were at 12 minute intervals during the night or off peak., although latterly only a few were used each day. North of the river most ran to or from Ferne Park or Brent. In the end most such trains came via the West London line which was much more economical with greater loads possible and no banking engines needed.

"The banking of trains up from Low Level with the associate 'crowing' of the train and banking engine whistles, and the engines pulling hard uphill, was very unpopular with the local business community, particularly since telephone conversations became impossible for a period on every train."

Mr W G Jackson of Guildford has been able to identify Tony Molyneaux's illustration of the working of No. 31806, page 30 of Issue No. 10. "I believe this to be the 5.16 pm Portsmouth and Southsea to Reading General. It was due to arrive on the up local at Basingstoke at 7.00 pm, then shunt to the East Bay and depart at 7.40 pm to Reading General. The duty number, 238, shown on the route discs is a Basingstoke turn. I do not have many sets of Engine Workings, but: 1959 Summer Service - Eastleigh Duty No. 273, diagrammed to work the 5.16 pm Portsmouth and Southsea to Reading General, BR Standard Class 4. This duty also diagrammed to work the 7.30 am Portsmouth and Southsea to Reading General earlier in the day. 1961 Summer Service: Basingstoke Duty No. 273. BR Standard Class 4, 5.16 pm Portsmouth and Southsea to Reading General."

Slightly late with Bill Jackson's next comment, as it refers to the piece on the Callington branch, Issue No. 7. "To contribute something towards the cost of maintaining the viaduct, a 'bonus mileage' was added to all rates on the branch. Distances were Bere Alston to;

Calstock	1m	55ch
Gunnislake	4m	47ch
Chilsworthy	5m	31ch
Latchley	6m.	39ch
Luckett	7m	58ch
Callington	9m	50ch

The bonus mileage of 2m 67ch was added to these. For charging purposes, distances were from buffer stops at the terminal, with intermediate stations being measured at the mid-point of the platforms."

Robert Latham, who kindly submitted some biographical details of his grandfather which appeared in issue 10, has also come up with another, rather more personal note. " I can recall my grandparents lived in Sandy Lane, Cheam. The family used to regularly visit by train to Norbury where we lived. I am told I got into trouble once as I had a dress-up guard's outfit and on one journey caused the train to depart from Sutton before it should!"

No sooner had Issue 11 hit the streets than we received a follow up from Tony Hillman reference the accident recounted to John Wale on Page 9. "John Wale - born Bideford 2nd quarter of 1871. 3 Apr 1881 census: living with his parents at 6 Railway Terrace, Bideford, his father, also John, was a Railway Horseman. 5 Apr 1891 census: in the Bideford Infirmary, occupation given as Porter. 31 Mar 1901 census: boarding with the Sing family at 10 Lime Grove Bideford, occupation given as Railway Warehouseman. 2 Apr 1911 census: living with his wife Lily, at 5 Brookfield Terrace, Bideford, occupation given as Warehouseman. The couple had married in 1904, but the only record of marriage I can find is of a John Wale to Lily Cook in Northampton. The year is correct 1904, but why Northampton? Lily was born in Hartland Devon in 1881. (Could it be someone did not approve of the match, hence the couple eloped - Ed?) John died in Bideford 3rd quarter 1935 age 64. Lily died in Bideford 4th quarter 1938 age 57. I can find no evidence of them having children. I can also find no reference of his death referred to in the 'Southern Railway' Magazine for 1935 or early 1936. Maybe he left the railway. Perhaps even in the 1911 census he was a Warehouseman but nothing to do with the Railway."

A regular friend of 'SW' is Fred Emery, who in a recent letter wrote, "….Whisper it quietly but I had forgotten the goods yard at Crawley and related my thoughts to Crawley New Yard - really at Three Bridges. The shot of Coulsdon North Sidings was again fascinating, especially with regard to the traffic of M A Rays' premises. On the left of the spread there are some electric coaches, quite a few of which appear to be the 2-car sets used to strengthen the 3SUBs into eight-car trains in peak times - or should that be rush-hours?" Fred continues concerning the 'Pull-Push / Push-Pull article in the same issue, "On the end of the nearest coach there is a large patch. With hindsight and prior to going to the IOW, these coaches were used on the Sheppey Light Railway and were gangwayed throughout to enable the Guard / Ticket collector to check and collect fares, was this patch over the remains of the connection?" then concerning station signage, "When did the use of a white background cease and the lettering become white instead…...sign writing is another dying art." Finally over Umberleigh and the vehicle on the forecourt, " the vehicle is an S & T department Thornycroft, quite popular with the WR who were then in charge of the station. The WR persisted with this type of vehicle long after other users were getting more mileage out of Austin, Bedford, BMC, and Ford amongst others." (Traditional signwriting is not dead yet, Rod Hoyle runs his own studio at 'Mill Signs' Romsey. I should also know better than try and produce a caption for a view with a road vehicle without asking Fred first - by the way, thanks for the lunch! Ed)

Eric Youldon is rightly quick to identify the various banana skins and similar that creep their way in from time to time. (Something about 'five-a-day' I read somewhere….ED). This time though he has kindly submitted a useful and informative addition to the recent debate on liveries. "Southern Post War Sunshine - One of the pleasures presented to the Southern enthusiasts in the early post-war years, was the return of a number of classes to lined malachite green livery. The 'King Arthurs' were honoured this way, the first being No. 776 'Sir Galagars', ex Eastleigh Works in March 1946. In July 1949 BR standard liveries were introduced, meaning lined dark green: which was basically the GWR livery for the likes of the 'Arthurs'. The final full repaint in malachite green for a member of the class was bestowed on No. 30786 'Sir Lionel' in early July 1949. naturally it was some time before malachite vanished on the type, the last to succumb to the BR green, No. 30743 'Lyonesse' in june 1953.

"The photograph features No. 30454 'Queen Quinevere' as turned out in malachite in March 1949, in which form it lasted until April 1951. The reason for the unmarked tender has been explained in SW No. 8, page 91." (Eric has kindly written with

No. 30454 'Queen Guinevere' in malachite, 19 March 1949.

Kindly submitted by John Cox, is this view of brand new No. 21C110, later given the name 'Sidmouth' on a local working in October / November 1945. At the time the engine was stationed at Redhill and was undertaking local train work between Redhill and Reading during which time coal and water consumption was being checked against the more usual 2-6-0 types used for passenger services on the route. The engine seen normally worked two return trips to Reading daily, the 7.43 a.m. and 5.36 pm out returning with the 12.17 pm and 9.34 pm respectively. It is seen here on what was most likely the 12.17 pm return, coming down the bank from Gomshall through Dorking Town around 1.30 pm.

observations on some of the illustration in the 'Wartime Southern' series. It is intended that these will appear in the final 'Wartime Southern Part 3' volume, scheduled - hopefully, for April 2011. ED)

Eric also identifies the mystery image of the train and signal box on page 95 of No. 9 - Honiton Incline Signal box.

Nothing to do with 'SW' how, but instead a note from Gerald Jacobs concerning one of our other books, 'A Chronology of the Constituent Locomotives of the Southern Railway.......'. "......At the outbreak of war in 1939, some withdrawn locomotives were 'rehabilitated'. Among these were several A12 'Jubilees' a veritable workhorse. At the end of the war we had to rapidly withdraw many doubly worn out engines and store them at places like Awbridge, which of course brought a lot of ribald comments in the press when we pleaded shortage of engines!"

Finally from Roger Morris of Finchley, with sincere apologies for failing to have used these wonderful memories before. "Having Herne Bay as my birthplace, it naturally followed that I would love all things Southern. Our family doctor was P Ransome-Wallis. It was almost worth being ill to enter his surgery, stuffed with various gauges of live-steam locomotive built by the doctor. These together with numerous photographs of trains adjourned the sides and walls. P Ransome-Wallis was already by this time acknowledged as one of the great railway authors and photographers: it has been my personal quest to collect a copy of all the books written by the man. We often wondered how he ever found time to cure his patients! (But cure them he did, without his expert intervention I would not be here today.)

"When allowed out from home, I was pushed by my mother to Cobblers Bridge, where I would watch for hours as a 'C' class 0-6-0 shunted, or observe the comings and goings of the four trains an hour. It seemed it was also a favourite place for the doctor, as many of his photographs were taken from the same spot.

"Come the time to select a grammar school, there was no contest. A bus journey to Canterbury, for the Simon Langton School, or by steam train to Faversham, for the Queen Elizabeth school.

"The usual engines for the service were 'Schools', either No. 30911 *'Dover'* or No. 30912 *'Downside'*, but in addition we had a wonderful selection of others over the years including 'Light Pacifics' and 'Q1s'. What surprises me is that over all he years this special school service operated there do not appear to be any photographs taken. It commenced from the island platform adjacent to Walker's coal yard - a site now unused and totally derelict. It was made up of eight coaches, four for the William Gibbs grammar school for girls and the others for us boys. There was a similar special working from Faversham in the afternoon.

"When I left school, I commenced work at Martin's bank in Lombard Street, using the 7.25 am to Cannon Street. My journey home , assuming I had balanced the books, was the fabulous 5.14 pm fast, first stop Whitstable. We always sat in the same seats on the up journey and it was often the case that if you were not going for any reason, no one else dared occupy it and it might remain empty for almost the whole journey. The restaurant car was also popular with the commuters, some using it daily to breakfast on the train."

- and speaking of Bulleids', they say beauty is in the eye of, and all that, but there is no one who could truthfully admit that the modification carried out to the front end of No. 34035 in 1959/60 were in any way appealing. Yes there was of course a serious side so far as what was almost the final attempt to reduce the incidence of drifting smoke which might well have had serious consequences for the forward vision of the driver. However, Mark Abbott's photograph, taken at Eastleigh clearly indicates much basic panel beating has taken place: to be fair, there was little alternative. As is known it was not a success and the engine reverted to conventional form. (See also the cover view of Issue 6.)

WINCHESTER: PART 2
Photographs submitted by Gerry Beale

Winchester Part 2? To be fair a second part on Winchester was never in the plan of things: that is we had used all of Rodney Youngman's material in Issue No. 11 and thought for the moment that might be it. But as chance would have it, a conversation with Gerry Beale on the topic of Winchester - mainly to advise him something was due shortly on what was for many years his own local station, evoked the comment, "I've got something on Winchester at home….I will bring it along next week.".

What transpired was an envelope of photographs taken in late August 1963 and recording the down side shortly before it was due to be modernised. This modernisation was in fact done piecemeal, although the result, approaching 50 years later, is a very different station wrapped around the same basic shell. For the sake of completeness and with apologies for squeezing out some other planned inclusions for this issue, a few pages of BR nostalgia. (Was it also that common to record what was soon to be swept away rather than new work?)

In photo No. 1, *the camera is pointing at the north end of the down platform: the 1960 signal box visible in the distance. The various barrows are in exactly the place they always were to receive mailbags that were brought to the station throughout the day from the sorting office by Royal Mail vans. The laden barrows were moved down the platform for loading into down passenger train or were wheeled across the barrow crossing at the north end of the platforms to the up side for loading into northbound trains. At the end of the building the notice on the wooden half gate proclaims 'Gentlemen Closed' with an arrow pointing to the left.*

Photo No. 2 *- The opposite end of the down platform. The brick hut was used by the p/way inspector. Notice in the distance the standard concrete oil hut: for safety well away from all other structures. Parallel with the railway at the top of the bank was the water tank used to feed the station water columns. (I once recall a chalked notice alongside the down water column, 'No water at Southampton'.) The pitched roof building at 90° to the railway was a drill hall.*

Photo 3 *- This is the down side entrance, with the twin set of steps leading down to the subway and access to the up platform, also the Stockbridge Road exit, thus saving an otherwise lengthy walk down the station approach and back under the Stockbridge Road bridge. In the evening there would queues outside the two 'T.K's, with city gents in bowler hats with rolled umbrellas and briefcases, phoning home to arrange their respective lifts. Taxis would also pull up by the edge of the pavement. Rodney's domain was around the edge of wall to the left: a well-worn wooden floor leading to the ticket windows. Anyone recalling the old Winchester will remember the hollow sound of those floorboards to this day.*

From a personal perspective, Photos 4 and 5 are probably the most interesting. **Photo 4** - is of course of the book stand: there was only this one on the down side, commuters for London being allowed to pass on to the platform, buy their daily paper, exit, and descend the steps to reach the up platform via the subway. It was here, when the structure was removed, that the ancient posters were discovered which Rodney referred to. As a child I often wondered how the man behind the counter got in and out....I never did find out. Gerry comments, "...I clearly remember buying copies of Trains Illustrated and Model Railway Constructor from the bookstall." To the left of the poster board was the door to the 'S.M.O.', more than one office in fact, and where Harry Hiller ended his railway career. (I recall as a schoolboy boldly walking into the office to ask the Station Master if I might have one of the signal arms removed with the installation of the first MAS in 1966: much of the station was otherwise little altered at that time. This was agreed and I followed the uniformed man to the site of the former 'up starter' and was presented with the stop arm, spectacle plate and spindle. He lifted it easily and I am sure hid a wry smile as I attempted, none too successfully, to emulate his effortless act. Getting it home was the next problem, we did not have a car. The option was the bus…….. "One and a signal to……". I got no further, as I was unceremoniously dumped by the conductress at the side of the road. I did get it home, how I cannot now recall, but it reposed in the garage for some years.)

Photo 5 - is of the entrance / exit with ticket collectors hut on the left. The metal sliding doors guarding the platform were only moved with some difficulty. The windows to the right face on to the booking hall, with the third, barred window, guarding the actual booking office. The clock, just visible on the extreme right, was a massive dark wood affair having two faces, I seem to recall it displayed the makers name of 'Walkers'. **Photo 6** - Here the camera has moved further south towards the Waiting and Ladies rooms - dark wooden furniture in the former (- I never went into the latter), and the refreshment room. Again just the single refreshment room on the down platform. Some terrible patterned wallpaper adorned the room, but the food and drink was palatable, served from a counter with glass display units situated on the left as one entered. (This was before the days the BR sandwich became the standard joke of most comedians.) Notice also the vertical case for the First-Aid stretcher, a common sight at SR Stations. I never saw it in use, although I did once witness a junior porter cross behind a stationary up train without realising a down express was bearing down. He made it, but only just, causing in the process a number of waiting passengers to have apoplexy. At the top of the photograph the valancing is that of the up platform and not some form of decoration.

Photo 7 - This is a continuation south with the double doors to the Parcels and Left Luggage office to the left. There was a similar double door on the opposite - approach side. The numerous poster boards were typical for the period, advertising both local and national enterprises. *Photo 8* - The set of double doors here gave access to the Parcels Office. Next came a staff room and finally the open door was the replacement Gentlemen's facilities - possibly formerly used just by staff but now serving the public as well. Just visible is the small covered shelter with limited accommodation for scooters and motorcycles, although as was seen earlier, ordinary bicycles were well catered for. On the 4-wheeled trolley are three oil lamps, one a hand lamp and two for the signals. The rear pitch of the canopy was glazed and consequently the platform itself was always light and airy. Standard green and white signs, southern lampshades, and as was seen in the other views, loudspeakers, complete the scene. *Photo 9* - This is the dead end at the south end of the station approach, at the time available for parking, but for many years now a through route. Previously, a footpath led up from the end of the pavement in the distance to the nearest roadway: Gladstone Street. Gerry recalls, "The footpath along the top of the cutting gave a splendid view of trains departing towards Southampton. I have the clearest recollections of a Urie S15 on a down freight coming to a stand at the down starter - it may have just finished shunting at Winchester - and then starting away towards Eastleigh and making a splendid noise!" The buildings at far left are long demolished, although out of camera to the left the 'South Western' public house still remains.

Gerry also submitted two other views, one was typical down train passing through the station and the other this delightful image, this time from the Roger Carpenter collection of M7 No. 30479 awaiting departure northbound in 1948. The service is probably an Alton working. The letter 'K' below the running number is the ex LSWR power classification introduced in Urie's time. It remained in use throughout Southern days and was continued into BR. In due course the ex LMS power classification was adopted and the M7s became class 2P.

Most trainspotters at Winchester would sit on the loading bank at the north end of the down platform. As Gerry comments, "One day I'll find a photo of a train entering Winchester and a view of myself at the same time"!

THE SOUTHERN 'STANDARD FIVES'

Keith Widdowson

Most enthusiasts are aware that the 20 Standard 5s delivered new to Stewarts Lane and Nine Elms during 1955, which acquired former 'King Arthur' class names four years later, will always be associated with the Southern Region. There were however, 25 further examples which at some time during their scandalously short lives could also claim to have played a part in moving the masses to and from the many seaside destinations along the English Channel coast. Keith Widdowson details their stay and recalls his own encounters with them.

Inspired by a recently read article of a Nine Elms fireman recalling his experiences of firing the "namers" out of Waterloo, I delved deep into my loft to research my own travels when chasing engines during the last few years of Southern steam. This led to an appreciation of just how much the BR Standard 5s played a significant part in transporting thousands of holidaymakers and commuters around the SR and that a grand total of 45 examples were, at some time during their existence, allocated to the Southern Region. In The BR Standard 4-6-0s 'Locomotive Illustrated' booklet, the following extract from the foreword by Derek Cross is worth restating - "It is only fair to single out the Southern Region (in comparison with other region's allocations) for special praise in getting the best out of the Standard 5s. Their best work in the south of England was probably done from Stewarts Lane and Nine Elms depots. At both depots the Standards took over from the 'King Arthurs' which, while exceptionally good engines, were long past their first youth by the mid-50s – some even taking their names!"

In comparison with other regions visited during their last years of steam, I personally noted that the domination of Standard BR designs (of all classes) was greater, as a proportion of the total steam stock, on the Southern than elsewhere. Perhaps the delayed implementation of the Bournemouth line electrification was too much to expect the ex-SR designs to last out for and, as this article will highlight, the authorities had no option but to gratefully receive displaced Standards from all over the country. Whilst the Standard 5s were inferior to the Southern Pacifics through smaller grate area and boiler capacity, they were superior hill climbers and more sure-footed from standing starts. Excluding the final batch of 'Merchants' (Nos, 35021-35030), ten members (Nos. 73110-73119) had the largest tenders on the region, specifically provided to compensate for the Southern's lack of water troughs and, taking into consideration all the foregoing, were "well-liked" by many enginemen.

The history, background, technical details and performance comparisons (particularly with the Black 5s), has been adequately documented in many publications by persons more knowledgeable than myself on such matters – I shall concentrate more on the allocations aspect and my own "catches" of these handsomely designed locomotives.

The Allocations

Nos. 73050-2 were the first brand new Standard 5s allocated to the SR at Bath Green Park (71G) in June 1954, but with the regional boundary changes in 1958, the former S & D north of Henstridge was transferred to the WR, resulting in both Bath Green Park and Templecombe sheds, crews and locomotives being lost to the WR. Nos. 73080 – 73086, built from June to August 1955, were allocated new to Stewarts Lane (73A) for use on the Kent Coast services and Nos. 73087-73089 & 73110-73119 (built August to December 1955) were delivered new to Nine

Opposite top - No. 73043 at Southampton Central with the 15.35 Waterloo to Bournemouth Central. We had arrived having had a tremendous ear-splitting run from the capital with this train. 1 April 1967.

Opposite bottom - Green liveried No. 73051 at Bournemouth West: my first run with a member of the class. The engine is preparing to depart with the 15.40 to Bristol TM on 9 May 1964. At the time this engine was allocated to Bath.

Right - Victoria, Sunday 13 November 1966, 'The West Country Special'. No. 73065 worked the outward leg via Herne Hill, Norwood Junction, Redhill and thence Reading to Westbury. From Westbury No. 34019 took over to Exeter St David's and Yeovil Junction with No. 35023 for the return to Waterloo.

No. 73117 (with replacement wooden smokebox numberplate) departing from Brockenhurst with the 11.30 Waterloo to Weymouth, 19 January 1966. I had alighted there to catch the connecting 12.20 departure for Lymington pier (seen on the right), which had 70F allocated, No. 80019 working the service.

Elms (70A) for the Bournemouth and Salisbury services – all eventually receiving names from former 'King Arthurs'. Stewarts Lane had all its nine engines (the original seven plus Nos. 73041 / 73042 sent from the LMR in exchange for 'Britannias' Nos. 70004 & 70014) transferred to Nine Elms in January 1960 upon implementation of phase one of the Kent Coast electrification (Chatham lines). With the arrival of Nos. 73167-73171 in the September of 1963, the maximum number ever allocated to the SR (39) was achieved – although this number was maintained for a mere eleven months.

Turning now to the individual shed allocations and starting at Nine Elms (70A). Here double figures were maintained (13-18) until August 1964, when four were transferred away together with two being withdrawn, falling to a low of one during the winter of 1965 / 1966. No doubt resulting from the whims of the locomotive diagrammers at the DMO Wimbledon, an increase to eight in May 1966 peaked with a high of ten during that summer before again returning to single figures until the end. Indeed the sole return Waterloo services booked for a 'Five' by April 1967 was the 04.40 to Salisbury and 18.38 return. Moving a few miles into the South West suburbs, the freight depot at Feltham (70B) received five from the NER in September 1963, rising three months later to eleven with transfers in from Eastleigh. All were taken away in November 1964, then for one month only – November 1965, Nos. 73016 / 73084 / 73085 were

allocated there. One may wonder did this one-month allocation actually take place, or was it simply a paper exercise?

Surrey's last remaining steam shed, Guildford (70C), didn't have any until May 1965 when eleven were transferred in (to supplement the gradually reducing ex-SR fleet of Moguls, Q & Q1 classes) from 70A / 70D, after which double figures were maintained for that year falling to single numbers from 1966 until the end – the class also playing a prominent part in the Bournemouth electrification infrastructure trains.

Eastleigh (70D), meanwhile, first received its allocation of three in March 1961, increasing in the August of that year with Nos. 73113 - 73119 arriving from 70A. An influx from the ER in December 1962, together with Feltham sending five in November 1964, further enhanced with three more in April 1965, courtesy of the WR, resulted in the most ever allocated to an SR shed (22) being achieved. This was soon reduced to single figures (December 1965) being maintained until the end. Finally to the end of the line at Weymouth (70G), which although never having had a double figure allocation and losing those in April 1967, still continued to use "visiting" Standard 5s right until the end on both passenger and freight traffic - in particular on the Westbury route. No Standard 5s were ever allocated to either Bournemouth (70F) or Salisbury (70E), although they were frequently seen there whilst visiting on other shed's duties. Now for a "did you know" fact - all the Standard 5s allocated to the SR ended their days on the region with one exception: No. 73167 which somehow escaped to the LMR (Shrewsbury) in August 1964.

Mention should also be made of the Standard 5s allocated to ex-SR sheds which, resulting from boundary changes in both 1958 and 1963, became part of the WR – these, however, are not being counted within the 45. Bath Green Park (71G/82F), although never exceeding a single figure allocation, was home to Nos. 73001, 73015, 73019, 73023, 73028, 73030, 73031, 73047, 73049, 73050, 73051, 73052, 73054, 73068, 73087, 73092, 73093 and 73164 at some time during their existence, working services over the former S & D route to Bournemouth – indeed on the three occasions when I visited the line in post 'Pines' days, it was awash with Standards of numerous classes. Exmouth Junction (72A / 83D) received Nos. 73030, 73044, 73161, 73162 and 73166 at various dates between September 1963 and January 1965 – the latter of which went on to Yeovil (72C/83E) until that shed's closure in June 1965. Although merely passing through Exeter twice during 1964, I fail to recall seeing any of them – nor indeed over the years have I seen photographs of them in action. Can any reader help as to which services did they work – or was it again a "paper" transfer: ie not actually taking place?

The Rail Tours

Retrospectively, I believe that the rail tour organisers were predisposed to utilising the fast disappearing pre-grouping / nationalised examples of the remaining steam fleet in preference to the "modern" Standards, and it was only towards the end of SR steam, when any steam locomotive was becoming of historic value, that greater use was made of them. My own travels included the use of No. 73065 (No. 73029 was failed through injector problems) between Victoria and Westbury on the SCTS "West Country Special" (13 November 1966), No. 73093 between Guildford and Waterloo on the LCGB "Hampshire Branch Lines Rail Tour" (9 April 1967), No. 73029 (with No. 76026 leading) between Weymouth and Bournemouth Central: incidentally attaining a lively 78mph approaching Worgret Jn, with the LCGB "Dorset Coast Express" (7 May 1967) and No. 73029 again this time leading No. 34023 *Blackmore Vale* between Waterloo and Fareham on the RCTS "Farewell to Southern Steam Tour" (18 June 1967). Researching on the www.sixbellsjunction.co.uk website, reveals that in the final few months the following classmates were also involved in tours – Nos. 73043, 73065 (31 December 1966), 73114 (30 April 1967) and 73085 (11 June 1967).

The Catches

Withdrawals of the class commenced in the February 1964 with No. 73027 on the WR, followed later that year with the Southern's Nos. 73046 and 73074. I had just started my travels that year, and as a consequence only caught runs with 36 out of the eventual 45 SR-allocated examples – and that includes Nos. 73050 & 73051 after their allocation away from the SR. Anticipating catching No. 73084 *Tintagel*, I left an appropriate space in my notebook for an entry – to no avail. I subsequently learnt never to document haulage until after actual movement had taken place - a practise still continued nowadays. A classic example of such naivety being a required Stanier, No. 44777, arriving into Basingstoke on the Poole - York one day, but after boarding the

train and redlining the number in my ever present Ian Allan Locoshed book, she was failed – with replacement No. 73093 departing some 45 minutes later! The other "namer" missed was No. 73116 *Iseult*. So what services did I catch my SR Standards on? My very first was a clean green-liveried, (as all WR allocated locos were "enhanced" after visiting Swindon for attention) No. 73051 out of Bournemouth West on an S & D service in May 1964. Regular evening outings from Waterloo to Woking on one of many steam-hauled commuter services often led to a return on the 15.00 from Bournemouth West (due Waterloo 18.26) service, which provided me runs with many of the named Nine Elms Standard 5s. Emphasising their versatility, three further Nine Elms examples were caught along the Redhill / Reading route just prior to dieselisation in the January of 1965. Waiting at Betchworth on the penultimate Saturday of steam along the route, I thought I had caught another one and only after thinking I had noted down a wrong number did it turn out to be No. 73028 of Oxley. What a sorry state she was in as well, with smokebox numberplate missing, rust all around the boiler and just a chalked number on the cab side the only form of identification. Mechanically she must have been better than she looked, for she was to last a further two years.

Another '5', and in a similar condition, was caught the following May, whilst bashing the Portsmouth / Cardiff services prior to their dieselisation the following month. Lifelong Nine Elms resident No. 73086 *The Green Knight* was caught working the Portsmouth portion of the Plymouth to Brighton, tender first from Fareham – the main train itself being worked through to Brighton with Eastleigh allocated No. 73110 *The Red Knight*. No. 73086 with all her number- and nameplates missing and rust everywhere, survived a further 15 months before withdrawal – showing again that you cannot judge a book by its cover. Another journey with *The Red Knight* two months later was enjoyed up the Pompey Direct, this time the diverted (because of engineering work) 19.20 Bournemouth West to Waterloo train. I had deliberately let the 18.20 departure via the normal route go, and waited for the novelty value of, at that time, a relatively rare route for normal booked steam haulage. At 123 miles, that was almost my longest single journey with a Standard 5 – the top prize going to ex-WR No. 73020 just two weeks later, when she worked through from Weymouth to Oxford (125¾ miles) on a Summer Saturday Wolverhampton-bound service. That was a good day for Standard 5 steam catches, having just arrived into Weymouth on the 05.30 from Waterloo with No. 73029 and out with No. 73020 – both required. The routing of the Wolverhampton service, via Yeovil, Melksham and Westbury. Enabled me to enjoy steam travel over lines unfamiliar to myself and, by then, steam free – excepting a sighting of a solitary pannier at Swindon. At that time Eastleigh Works still dealt with repairs and overhauls to steam from other regions, which would occasionally be reported on SR services "running in" before being returned home. The only time I chanced across such an event was on a foggy night in November 1965, when Caprotti No. 73133 (9H – Patricroft) worked the 18.35 Salisbury to Waterloo. Again, similar to No. 73028 previously mentioned, I thought I had misread the number at Woking and had to confirm it at Waterloo; not, at the time, being sufficiently knowledgeable enough to notice the valve gear variations. A side effect of chasing steam in this fashion, was an

Usually the preserve of a Nine Elms Class 3MT, No. 73170 is seen departing Waterloo on 28 January 1966 with the 14.10 Milks to Kensington Olympia.

increased geographical knowledge of Britain – reference to an atlas upon returning home had revealed the location of the previously unheard of Mancunian suburban depot mentioned above. Visiting Caprotti sister engine No. 73130 was noted a few weeks later at Eastleigh but alas never caught.

Although often noted on the Bournemouth semis and the York trains, the main catches had to be on the commuter services out of Waterloo, in the evenings particularly. Taking into consideration that the 17.23 FO and the 18.09 SX departures were booked for Standards, together with the returning 20.29 arrival from Salisbury, this would often, during the Spring and Summer of 1966, regularly lead to up to four in circulation. The 17.09 Waterloo to Basingstoke although usually a Bulleid, was not immune to Standardisation and on one cold January evening in 1967 a welcome invite for a footplate ride between Woking and Winchfield was offered by Driver Sacree (70D) on No. 73087 *Linette* – one of four engines of the class especially reinstated for the Xmas parcels extra traffic. It was withdrawn (for the second and final time) three days later. Woking (because of Guilford's closeness) and Basingstoke (because of its stabling point) were the engine-changing locations for ailing locomotives on main line services and more often than not the 5s came to the rescue, ie No. 73018 from No. 76058 on the Down Mails in January 1967, and No. 73043 from No. 75074 on the evening Salisbury in June 1967. The 5s, however, were not immune to problems themselves – two examples being No. 73171 being replaced by D6538 on the 17.09 Waterloo and 34036 from No. 73092 at Eastleigh on the 07.23 Bournemouth to Waterloo service, both in April 1967. The latter was on a Saturday morning, and having departed Waterloo on the 17.23 service the previous day and then doubled back for the 22.35 and the 02.45 services overnight, I eventually departed Waterloo for the third time within 22 hours with No. 73043 on the 15.35 semi. Initially disappointed with collecting a run with a Standard instead of a Bulleid, Driver Ward

(70F) gave her some "wellie" and with rapid accelerations from all the calling points en route, created a fantastic raucous exhaust which must have been heard miles from the line, also more than maintaining time with the nine vehicle train – without excessive speeding. Not expecting any recordable performance, I failed to document it – fatigue taking its toll! Indeed I was fortunate to be on board during some very creditable performances, ie No. 73029 with a load of ten on the 17.09 Waterloo (7 October 1965), taking 27m 44s to Woking with a maximum of a mere 70mph after Weybridge: No. 73133 with a load of seven on the 18.35 Salisbury (18 November 1965) in from Woking in 27m 57s with a max of 71mph approaching Hersham, and finally the maximum speed I ever recorded with the class - 82½ mph at Brookwood – this time with No. 73065 on the same train (8 February 1967), and with Driver Thompson of 70A.

By early 1967, the condition of all the remaining steam locomotives on the Southern Region would have caused today's health and safety officials to have heart attacks. Run down, worn out, filthy, coated with a thick covering of oil, number / name/ shed plates missing and being sent out by foremen having their fingers crossed - a definite wing and a prayer job. The Bulleids received greater attention in respect of cleanliness - often the only identifying feature on a Standard 5 being the cabside number having been cleaned - just in that area. Eastleigh fitter Ron Cover, treated two of them with his "soup can" numberplate replacements – No. 73029 given gold numbers on a black backdrop and No. 73155 white numbers on a red backdrop. As primarily a Bullied fan, the frequent replacement by Standard 5s on passenger services wasn't, as first thought, a vendetta against us, it was just that the Standards (perhaps being newer and with more easily accessible components) fared better than the older Bulleids in coping with the reduced maintenance and overhauls given them. Although contributing towards an exciting if sad time, the authorities, already despairing at the months of delay to the inaugu-

It was the final day of the nearby Fawley branch passenger services and a flying fill in visit to Lyndhurst Road was made. No 73170 (again) is seen departing on 11 February 1966 with the 14.02 Eastleigh to Bournemouth Central.

ration of the electrified services (stock delivery), must have been at their wits' end in attempting to keep the trains running.

My own best months for "new" catches were in September 1965 and February 1966 with four each month – indeed I was fortunate in getting No. 73111 *King Uther* on the Down Mails a mere nine days before her withdrawal. No. 73002 was my final "need", being caught whilst working a stopping service through the New Forest in May 1966. Summing up my catches and my mileage behind the class, the figures obviously pale into insignificance when compared to the Bulleids. Whenever the choice was there, usually the Bulleid won, because not only were they more powerful (7P5F versus 5MT) but with the "gung ho" mentality of certain drivers in the final year, three figure speeds were often attained. Even so, the 5,535 miles behind 77 members of the class I have travelled comprised a respectable 63% behind the 36 allocated to the SR.

The Last Week

This final sad week of SR steam has been well documented over the years, particularly with anniversary date issues of steam-orientated magazines. Allow me therefore to merely extract the known passenger workings of the survivors of which only eight out of the remaining eleven were in action. Taken in numerical order, No. 73018 (fresh from working the final steam service over the North Downs route the previous month), was sent out by Weymouth on the 08.27 to Bournemouth on the Friday, being returned 48 hours later on the final day's only Standard working – the 10.02 return service to Weymouth. On Monday 3 July, Weymouth sent out No. 73020 on the 10.13 to Bournemouth – then worked the 15.01 return and finally the 18.15 Weymouth to Waterloo. Nine Elms quickly turned her out for the 02.45 papers to Bournemouth; but resulting from a failure of No. 34102 *Lapford,* she was stepped up for the 02.30 Pompey papers instead – returning to Eastleigh on the workers' service from Fratton. Former WR green-liveried No. 73029 was noted on the Tuesday with the 16.20 Southampton to Bournemouth before making her way to Weymouth for the following day's

10.13 to Bournemouth. Next appearing in the early hours at Waterloo on the 02.45 Bournemouth papers, I declined her (even though the speed merchant Driver Porter was in charge), in order to obtain the prestigious 1,000 miles behind the 02.30 locomotive – No. 34036 *Westward Ho*. No. 73029 continued to Weymouth that morning, returning to Bournemouth on the 16.47 service later that day. The Friday saw her work into Salisbury on the 16.51 from Basingstoke, before taking Salisbury's own final steam departure – the 18.38 to Waterloo. No. 73037's only move of the week was on the 17.16 Southampton to Bournemouth on the Monday, as was sister No. 73043 on the Friday. No. 73065 also only appears to have worked one passenger service that week – the 15.55 Salisbury to Basingstoke on the Tuesday. No. 73092 was late on the scene, being reported on the 08.35 Waterloo to Weymouth on the Thursday, returning to London for Friday's 02.45 papers continuing through to Weymouth on the 07.08 service before bowing out with the final Saturday 12.12 Weymouth to Bournemouth service. This three coach stopper was "jammed to the gunwales" by enthusiasts, (myself included), having just arrived in on the last steam service out of Waterloo – No. 35023 *Holland Afrika Line* on the Channel Isles boat train. Finally No. 73093's only reported passenger workings of that week were Monday's 07.18 Waterloo to Salisbury and the 15.55 from there to Basingstoke.

In summary it may be stated that the SR Standard 5s provided a useful backup for the superior Bulleids (No. 73043 being observed on the Down Bournemouth Belle on 8 May 1967); consequently, by their own versatility I suspect, remaining until the end – with two (Nos. 73050 and 73082) surviving into preservation. This article has been compiled primarily from my own observations but has also been enhanced from material periodically purchased (and kept much to my wife's consternation) – but is not necessarily comprehensive. If you know different / more, please forward details to me via the editor. I hope that the memories are revisited for those readers who, like myself, were "fortunate" to witness the death of SR steam

Date	Caught	Withdrawn	Surviving	Remaining required	Remarks
1957			23	-	73050-2,73080-9, 73110-9
1959			27 (A)	-	73017/8 ex ER, 73020/2/9 ex WR, 73041/2 ex LMR, 73050-2 to WR
12/62			34	-	73002/16/43/6/65/74 ex ER 73155 ex NER
09/63			39	-	73167/8/9/70/1 ex NER
01/64			39	39	
08/64		73046/74	36	36	73167to LMR
09/64	73080	73017	35	34	
10/64	73112		35	33	
11/64	73085/110	73116	34	30	
12/64	73115/9		34	28	
01/65	73089		34	27	
02/65	73082		34	26	
04/65			37	29	73037/92/3 ex WR
05/65	73086		37	28	
06/65		73041/112	35	27	
07/65	73020/9/117		35	24	
08/65		73042	34	23	
09/65	73022/111/3/69	73111	33	19	
11/65	73155/68		33	17	
12/65	73081/3/114/70	73084/168	31	12	
01/66	73037/87/118		31	9	
02/66	73016/65/93/171		31	5	
03/66	73018/43/88		31	2	
05/66	73002/92		31	0	
06/66		73082/114/70	28		
07/66		73081	27		
09/66		73083/9	25		
10/66		73086/7/8/169/71	20		
12/66		73016/80	22		73087/8/9/169 returned to traffic 12/12/66 – 07/01/67
01/67		73110/3	16		
03/67		73002/115/7/9	12		
04/67		73022	11		
07/67		73018/20/9/37/43/ 65/85/92/3/118/55	0		

Notes to table above -

(A) – 73087 was loaned to Bath Green Park (82F) 06/60 – 08/61
Withdrawn at 70A – 73022/9/37/43/6/65/74/85/6/112   (10)
        70C – 73018/20/41/81/2/7/8/9/92/3/110/5/7/8/55 (15)
        70D – 73084/111/6/9/68/9/70/1   (8)
        70G – 73002/16/7/42/80/3/113/4   (8)
        Transferred away 73050/1/2/167   (4)
                                ----
                             (45)

Notes to table on opposite page -
(A) – 73087 was loaned (from Nine Elms) to Bath Green Park (82F) 06/60 – 08/61
(B)– Eastleigh was coded 71A until 09/63
(C)– Weymouth was coded 71G until 09/63
(D) - 73087/8/9/169 returned to traffic 12/12/66 – 07/01/67 at 70C
(E)– Shed transferred to WR (82F) in 1958

THE RAILWAY CORRESPONDENCE AND TRAVEL SOCIETY
THE SOUTHERN RAILWAYMENS HOME FOR CHILDREN

FAREWELL TO SOUTHERN STEAM TOUR

SUNDAY, 18th JUNE, 1967

WATERLOO · EAST PUTNEY · COBHAM · GUILDFORD · HASLEMERE
FAREHAM · NETLEY · SOUTHAMPTON · LYNDHURST ROAD
BOURNEMOUTH · WAREHAM · SWANAGE · WEYMOUTH
POOLE · EASTLEIGH · SALISBURY · BASINGSTOKE · WATERLOO

THE SOUTHERN STANDARD FIVES

Date	70A Nine Elms	70B Feltham	70C Guilford	70D (B) Eastleigh	70G (C) Weymouth	71G (E) Bath G Park	73A Stew Lane	Total
1957	13					3	7	23
1959	13				5		9	27
1960	19 (A)				8			27
03/61	18			3	5			26
04/61	18			2	6			26
08/61	12			7	8			27
12/62	14			12	8			34
09/63	14	5		11	9			39
12/63	13	11		9	6			39
08/64	7	10		12	7			36
09/64	7	9		14	5			35
11/64	9			19	6			34
04/65	9			22	6			37
05/65	4		11	16	6			37
06/65	3		10	16	6			35
09/65	2		10	15	6			33
10/65	1	3	13	9	7			33
11/65	1		13	11	8			33
12/65	1		13	9	8			31
05/66	8		9	6	8			31
06/66	10		8	4	6			28
07/66	10		7	4	6			27
09/66	10		6	4	5			25
10/66	6		6	3	5			20
12/66	6		5 (D)	2	5			22
01/67	6		5	2	3			16
03/67	6		3	1	2			12
04/67	5		6					11
07/67								0

Shed Allocations

No. 73170 at Eastleigh Platform 3 having arrived with the 09.30 Waterloo to Bournemouth Central. 11 December 1965.

Acknowledgements:
www.steamsheds.co.uk: John Bird's *Southern Steam Surrender:*
www.kentrail.co.uk:
Locomotives Illustrated BR Standard 5s (Ian Allan)

Top - *The 'New' control office at Southampton. In the foreground is Mr A. 'Bing' Crosby dealing with the Motive Power Panel, centre is Mr R. Cale: the Deputy Chief Controller, and in the background, Guards Inspector, Mr. D Lickman. In the right background is Mr A Senior, who during the night hours covered both areas 2 and 4. (This was from Totton west through to Weymouth, including all branches, and north to Alderbury Junction and Sparkford but excluding the S & D. A map of the areas covered by the various sections appeared in the first instalment of this series.)*

Left - *3.00 p.m., Thursday 30 June 1960. WR 0-6-0PT No. 1368 with the stock for the 15.45 Weymouth Quay to Waterloo.*

LIFE AT SOUTHAMPTON TSO

Richard Simmons

Part 3: Specific Routes and Traffic Flows

Continuing on with this very popular series on life at the Southampton Train Supervision Office, 'Control', from the mid 1950s onwards.

Previous instalments appeared in Issues 6 and 8 of 'Southern Way'. More will follow shortly.

Cross Channel Shipping Services

Two services operated to the Channel Islands, comprising the ex-GWR from Weymouth and SR from Southampton. As regards the actual distance by sea, the GWR route was shorter, but initially the TSO had no involvement with associated boat trains to and from Paddington - until transfer of the Castle Cary - Weymouth line to the SR. However, from the 1959 winter timetable, these trains ran to and from Waterloo.

A furor erupted when, from May 1961, all Channel Islands services were concentrated on Weymouth. At that time Southampton regarded itself as Britain's premier passenger port, and this move was a dent to the town's (Southampton had not achieved city status then) pride. I recall the local evening newspaper being very vociferous in its condemnation of the transfer which also had some teething troubles. The up afternoon boat train, booked to depart Weymouth Quay at 16.00, could if running late delay the 16.45 Weymouth - Bournemouth Central stopper and if necessary had to pass the slower train at Dorchester South, after it had reversed into the up platform. Following a few occurrences of this nature, regular 16.45 passengers complained. As the then South of England Branch editorial representative of the RCTS, I submitted a report about this unsatisfactory situation and a note duly appeared on p. 256 of the August 1961 'Railway Observer' - 'RO'. By some means unknown to me the aforementioned newspaper gained access to this report, which gave grist to its campaign mill and in turn slated the transfer. The morning after the newspaper report was printed, the CTC was not best happy about it, storming and ranting into the TSO wondering who had written the RO report; 1 happened to be on duty and kept my head down!

Summer Saturday afternoons were particularly difficult with up train working, there being four Waterloo-bound trains scheduled to depart in the space of 90 minutes from the three Weymouth Quay platforms. In addition, a portion with through carriages to Cardiff and Birmingham Snow Hill was worked to Weymouth Jct., for attachment to a through train to Birmingham from Weymouth Town. Other causes of delay on the Quay tramway were from parked cars on the roadway obstructing the railway and flooding from high Spring tides when water came up through drains.

Seasonal Channel Islands cut flower traffic often required special van trains. For instance, on Good Friday, 4 April 1958, two such trains ran from Southampton Old Docks: at 20.38 non-stop to Waterloo and formed as follows; vans for Kew Bridge and Waterloo, then vans for Glasgow, Preston, Liverpool, Manchester, Crewe, and Coventry via Clapham Junction and Willesden - this portion to have a brake van. The rear portion being comprised of vans for Doncaster, Leeds Central, Hull, Newcastle and Edinburgh via Clapham Junction and Kings Cross. Vehicles in the rear portion had to be 'in gauge' to pass over the Metropolitan widened lines to Kings Cross. The two portions routed via Clapham Junction formed a special from Waterloo to Clapham Junction.

The second special departed the Old Docks at 21.35 for Crewe, with traffic for and via Basingstoke and the WR. After the transfer to Weymouth there was a regular 18.45 Weymouth Quay - Bristol TM parcels train.

Meanwhile back at Southampton cross-channel services were not quite dead, the Le Havre service lingering until March 1964, albeit operating only on three days per week in mid-winter, being catered for by a portion detached from the rear of the 19.30 Waterloo-Bournemouth West at Southampton Central. Finally, the summer St. Malo boat service ceased at the end of the 1965 summer season.

Pigeon Traffic

South coast destinations were quite a favourite amongst pigeon fanciers for release of their birds. Some very lengthy van trains from various starting stations in the Midlands and north of England (and, if I recall correctly, the occasional train from Scotland) came our way, many notoriously bad timekeepers! Trouble invariably arose on Saturday mornings, when the pigeons were due for release but prevented from doing so by wet weather or strong winds; sea fog hugging the coast also prevented flying. If such weather continued into Saturday evenings, return trains conveying empty pigeon baskets were consequently delayed, in turn requiring train crew revision

Hampshire Strawberry Traffic

This was centred principally on the area surrounding Botley, Swanwick and Bursledon stations. I don't know how many of these former strawberry fields survive today but suspect many must now be beneath bricks and mortar, or even the M27. I had little to do with this traffic, not working regularly on No. 3 area, but special van trains departed from these stations during

early evenings in June and July often making the long trek to north of England and Scottish destinations as well as to London; empty vans worked in during the mornings. Being perishable, some priority had to be given to these trains. A separate special traffic notice was published for this traffic detailing timings, train formations and how van interiors were to be loaded. To my regret, I did not retain a copy of any such notices.

Milk Traffic

In the district, this traffic was confined to the S&D, and limited to just two milk trains. On weekdays they were 16.40 Wincanton - Templecombe (worked by a light engine from Templecombe) and 16.45 Bailey Gate - Templecombe, worked by engine and stock off the 15.34 Templecombe - Bailey Gate passenger. Whilst the S&D might generally slumber on winter Sundays the cows did not, so certain signal boxes had to open for a light engine, Templecombe – Wincanton, returning with the 15.30 Wincanton - Templecombe. At Templecombe loaded tanks were attached to the up Seaton Jct.-Clapham Jct. milk train. So at Southampton, the TSO only heard anything about these trains from Bath control if anything went wrong.

Channel Island Tomato Traffic

On my first early turn on the newly created No.4 area, following transfer of the Castle Cary-Weymouth line to the SR, the Weymouth yard inspector telephoned at about 07.30 to give the yard position. He then started talking in what seemed a foreign language by referring to 'toads', 'perpots' and 'venlos'! I was well aware that a toad was an ex-GWR design freight brake van with large verandah at one end, but must confess ignorance about perpots and venlos. This gap in my education of railway terminology arose from the fact that the SR did not use the telegraphic codes used by other regions, and I soon learned that perpot was the code for a C1.4 special train conveying perishable traffic. In this case the term was used for Channel Islands tomato trains front Weymouth. Venlo was the code used for special empty trains, which in this case referred to trains of empty vanfits to Weymouth.

But back to that first early turn, in retrospect I think the SR was initially ill prepared to deal with this traffic, but very soon got its act together and perpot timings and formations were soon published in the SR tidy manner in special traffic notices. They were later included in the WTT from summer 1959 onwards. Also from 1959, a separate pamphlet - SR published - was produced detailing all instructions, marshalling and timings for these trains. The WR and GWR had long produced such a publication - I have a photocopy of the 1901 GWR notice. The daily procedure was as follows: between 07.00 and 07.30, the Weymouth yard inspector telephoned us with details of each train formation and agreed any deviation necessary according to daily requirements. We in turn advised WR Westbury control. Upon departure of each train from Weymouth yard, yard staff advised us of the time of departure, engine number and actual formation. In turn, these details were also relayed to Westbury control. There were no tomato pickings on Guernsey on Sundays and consequently no trains ran on Mondays. The season lasted from about May until mid-October and naturally during the shoulder peaks in early and late season, all trains did not run.

Taking the 1961 season for example, specials from Weymouth were as follows (all Mondays excepted): 09.05 to York via Westbury, thence the Berks & Hants line to Newbury, via the DN&SR to Didcot, and then Oxford, Banbury, Woodford and the GCR. This service was actually two trains conjoined, each having its own brake van, hence the sight of a brake van in the middle of the train. Upon being split by the Eastern Region, one section was worked forward with traffic for the Scottish Region via Berwick, the other section was for Hunberside, York and Newcastle.

After this came the 09.55 to Crewe (Gresty Lane): via Westbury, Berks & Hants line, Newbury, DN&SR to Didcot, Oxford, Birmingham (Snow Hill), Wellington and Market Drayton; conveyed traffic for Leamington Spa, West Midlands, Derby, via Oxley sidings, LMR and Scottish regions. 10.20 to Saltney: via Westbury, Dr. Day's Bridge Jct., Severn Tunnel Jct, Hereford and Shrewsbury; conveyed traffic for Newport - Shrewsbury line stations, Chester, North Wales, Birkenhead, Liverpool (Edge Hill) and Manchester (Liverpool Road). 15.00 to Cardiff: via Westbury, Dr. Day's Bridge Jct. and Severn Tunnel Jc;. conveyed traffic for south Wales. 16.55Q to Crewe: same route as 09.55; conveyed traffic for LMR, ER, NER and ScR destinations.

Needless to say on Summer Saturdays evening departures were the rule and a different programme applied on Sundays. Engines shown were Halls which in later years were replaced by Std. Class 5

Private and not for Publication.

SOUTHERN

BRITISH RAILWAYS
(SOUTHERN REGION)

INSTRUCTIONS FOR WORKING

PERISHABLE TRAFFIC
(EX CHANNEL ISLANDS)

FROM

WEYMOUTH (Quay)
At Freight Train Rates.

SEASON 1961

IT IS IMPORTANT THAT TRAINS CONVEYING PERISHABLE TRAFFIC SHOULD MAINTAIN THEIR SCHEDULES. THESE SERVICES MUST START PUNCTUALLY, AND ALL CONCERNED ARE REQUESTED TO GIVE THE WORKING SPECIAL ATTENTION.

CONNECTING SERVICES FOR TRAFFIC CONVEYED BY ORDINARY TRAINS ARE LAID DOWN IN THIS NOTICE, AND EVERY EFFORT MUST BE MADE TO MAINTAIN THEM.

(BR31404/2)
1544

A. EARLE EDWARDS,
Operating Officer,
Waterloo.

Opposite page - C2X No. 32548 on what was officially referred to as a 'Short Notice Special', seen here between Netley and Sholing. The circumstances were that a solitary tank car scheduled to travel, had been left behind at the Hamble oil terminal sidings by a previous train. This special working was sent out to collect it. Regulations also required the tank car have the requisite two barrier wagons from the engine and also the brake-van. 26 March 1959.

Right - In March 1960 information was received that the turntable at Salisbury would soon be out of commission for repair / replacement. Consequently with the potential for WR locomotives arriving on through workings from Westbury unable to turn, arrangements were made to see if members of the 'Hall' class could satisfactorily work through to Portsmouth via Southampton. This necessitated a special gauging train being run on Tuesday 15 March 1960, seen here as the 10.30 Fareham - Bevois Park with measurements being taken at Sholing. The engine is No. 4917 'Crosswood Hall.'

4-6-0s. Maximum loads were 42 fully fitted wagons and brake van but the 09.25 to York was permitted 46. The minimum load for trains to run was 15 and when below this number, some trains were combined.

Ordinary freight services also conveyed tomato traffic and if 10 wagons or more were offered, an 18.55 to Nine Elms ran. If between six and nine wagons, then the train ran to Southampton Old Docks where they were forwarded on the 22.30 thence to Nine Elms.

With regard to venlos, the Western District seemed to round-up empty vanfits for two trains of 40 wagons each departing Yeovil Jct. at 00.01 and 22.40 for Weymouth. Both trains required two brake vans for the double reversal at Yeovil Town and Yeovil Pen Mill. The 22.40 had to be reduced to a single engine load at Yeovil Pen Mill for the climb of Evershot bank, whilst the 00.01 was made up there to banked engine load. During the morning the Freight stock department advised us whether one or both venlos were required the following night and if only one was required, the TSO cancelled the other.

Banana Traffic

This consisted of Elders & Fyffes fruit trains, running from Southampton Old Docks in conjunction with their requirements. The Freight (TG) section prepared programmes which lasted over about three days. Whilst most trains used the Q pathways in the freight WTT, some special pathways were arranged. Programmes detailed each train's formation, as well as wagon destinations conveyed on ordinary services. The docks advised departure time of each train and details of any deviation from the arranged programme. The TSO passed on this information to the next control concerned, usually Woking or for DN&SR routed trains, WR Reading. From time to time special trains were cancelled at short notice due to problems within the docks, such as a stevedore shortage which arose especially when a "Queen" liner docked, or mechanical problems with the unloading equipment or even industrial action. It should be remembered that at the time, industrial relations in the country's docks could be rather volatile. When cancellations occurred, apart from advising motive power depots concerned, guard's and the next control area, the TSO advised the TG section to enable them to liaise with Elders & Fyffes for replacement trains.

Fawley Oil Trains

The story of this intriguing branch is admirably told in the late John Fairman's excellent book *The Fawley Branch* (published by the Oakwood Press). Suffice it to say here, the line opened as the Totton, Hythe & Fawley Light Railway in 1925. From timetable perusal over the years, one can be forgiven for concluding that passenger traffic was never heavy, there being no more than 3-4 weekday trains which became even fewer in the years preceding withdrawal of passenger trains from 14 February 1966. A meagre Sunday service was provided, consisting of one train each way and geared for refinery workers, to Fawley in the early morning, returning late afternoon. These were unadvertised until the 1954 winter timetable. During construction of the oil refinery, circa 1950, (although there was a small plant beforehand), large numbers of construction workers had to be conveyed down in the morning, returning late afternoon / early evening. To increase accommodation on these trains, what was probably the most bizarre sight could be seen in the form of close-coupled six-wheeled coaches borrowed from the LMR. Before I worked in the TSO, I was in the divisional office, commercial section, and

Opposite top - *'N15' No. 30771 'Sir Sagramore' on the up through line just south of Shawford with the 16.25 Southampton Old Docks to Temple Mills special banana train. 6 June 1960.*

Opposite bottom - *A 'Nelson' on freight. No. 30858 'Lord Duncan' on the last leg of the 02.30 Ashford to Eastleigh freight, running on the down relief line just south of Shawford. 21 July 1958.*

Right - *'H16' 4-6-2T No. 30517 on a short working, the 12.50 Eastleigh to Northam Yard. The train is seen passing St Denys with the junction for the Fareham route, via Netley, on the right. 4 January 1961.*

Left - 34009 'Lyme Regis' crossing Canute Road, Southampton with the 09.21 Waterloo - Southampton Old Docks, 29 April 1959.

Opposite page - Banking duty for No. 34090 'Sir Eustace Missenden Southern Railway.' The train is the 21.50 Swansea to Brockenhurst recorded between Parkstone and Branksome at 16.10 on 18 August 1962. Notice the missing tail lamp.

every fortnight worked a Saturday turn finishing at 12.00. This was in 1951/52 during the time when on the first Saturday afternoon of each month there were regular monthly visits by the RCTS to Eastleigh locomotive works and MPD. When my Saturday turn coincided with such visits, I travelled from Southampton Central to Eastleigh on the 12.14SO Fawley - Eastleigh to ensure I rode in these venerable coaches.

Oil traffic burgeoned through the late 1950s early 1960s, during which time production of town gas switched from coal / coke to oil. Taking the summer 1962 freight WTT as an example and when this traffic was probably at its height, loaded tank car train departures from Fawley were as follows;

01.15 MXQ to Tiverton Jct.: via Chandlers Ford and Salisbury; block train of fourteen tank cars, four runners and two brake vans; engine change at Eastleigh station.

04.10MX (from 2 October 1962) to Bromford Bridge: via DN&SR; block train of 25 tank cars, four runners and brake van; engine change at Eastleigh No. 1 up goods.

09.10 (from 7 January 1963) to Denham: via Basingstoke; block train of sixteen tank cars, four runners and two brake vans; DL hauled.

13.00SX (from 4 March 1963) to Spondon / Leicester: via DN&SR; block train of 30 tank cars, four runners and brake van; engine change at Eastleigh No.1 up goods.

1320SO/13.40SX to Bevois Park sidings: tank cars for various destinations plus general traffic. 14.20SX to Bromford Bridge: via DN&SR; block train of 25 tank cars, four runners and brake van; engine change at Eastleigh No.1 up goods.

14.20SOQ to Eastleigh marshalling yard: block train of 25 tank cars, four runners and brake van; formed 00.40MOQ Eastleigh to Bromford Bridge.

17.45SO to Eastleigh marshalling yard: block train of 24 tank cars, four runners and brake van plus ordinary traffic; Denham tank cars forwarded on 12.15MO Eastleigh to Denham.

19.10SX to Eastleigh marshalling yard: tank cars for various destinations plus general traffic; retimed to start 18.40 from 4 February 1963.

20.30SX to Northampton: via DN&SR; block train of fourteen tank cars, four runners and brake van;. engine change at Eastleigh No.1 up goods; retimed to start 21.20 from 1 April 1963.

22.00SX to Denham: via Basingstoke; block train of sixteen tank cars, four runners and brake van each end; engine change at Eastleigh No.1 up goods.

23.15SX to Bromford Bridge: via DN&SR; block train of 25 tank cars, four runners and brake van each end; engine change at Eastleigh No.1 up goods.

The introduction of roller bearing tank cars from early 1963 enabled more vehicles to be conveyed.

Fawley gave the TSO details of those tank car destinations conveyed on ordinary trains, which in turn were passed on to Bevois Park and Eastleigh yards as forwarding services were laid down. In following years block trains ran to other destinations but the decline started about the 1970s, long after my time in the TSO. This decline was largely due to construction of underground pipe lines and closure of town gas works as North Sea natural gas came on line: a commodity we are now told is running out! The principal operating problem of this branch arose from the fact that with no turntable at Fawley, tender first running in one direction was unavoidable and with increasing loads larger locomotives were essential. Some, such as the Qls, had enclosed cabs thereby impairing vision of the ungated level crossings on the branch, many of which were equipped with barriers as the years went on. A partial solution to this problem was the use of tank engines and at first ex-LB&SCR E4 and E6 0-6-2Ts were drafted in which from 1952 were replaced by Ivatt C1. 2 and Std. Cl. 3 2-6-2Ts. Larger tank engines were also tried, such as H16 4-6-2T, W 2-6-4Ts and Z 0-8-0Ts but all were swept away by the coming of Cl. 33 diesels from 1963. As loads increased, that on

the 19.10 Fawley often exceeded a single engine load requiring an assisting engine. This request, usually made during the afternoon, often caused problems at Eastleigh MPD due to shortage of footplate crews. However, the Freight (TG) section soon realised the problem and arranged with the Waterloo engine diagram section to permanently roster a second engine. On the occasions the second engine was not required, Fawley advised the TSO who cancelled it. Such advice was necessary fairly early in the afternoon to prevent the engine leaving the MPD from where, if it had already escaped, signal boxes had to be contacted to establish its whereabouts and arrangements made to stop it at a suitable point and advise the crew to return to Eastleigh. The 13.00 Fawley also had the services of an assisting engine, having run light from Millbrook yard.

The ungated level crossings required running under great caution with corresponding slow speeds and much locomotive whistling. At the time I lived in one of Southampton's suburbs on the east side of Southampton Water and, when on early turn in the TSO and leaving home at 06.30, if the wind was in the right direction as I cycled along could easily hear the wail of the Std. Cl. 3 2-6-2T's whistle from the other side of the water as it made its way cautiously towards Fawley on the 04.06 ex-Eastleigh freight. On occasions a Stanier hoot was heard indicating that it was an Ivatt 'Mickey Mouse' 2-6-2T.

The coming of the Bromford Bridge block trains required adequate motive power once clear of the Fawley branch. This came in the form of Std. Cl. 9F 2-10-0s of which initially none were allocated to the SR. Instead the 9Fs used were LMR provided and, if I recall correctly, the actual engine workings showed them as being Saltley duties. However, problems arose when the LMR did not provide a 9F, for whilst several other classes of engine could haul the empties down, they might be totally unsuitable to work a return loaded train, thus requiring a juggling of engine power. One such occasion brought a 'Royal

Scot' to the south coast in March 1962: No. 46141 *The North Staffordshire Regiment* brought an empty train south but could not return to the LMR on a loaded train. The locomotive was returned 'home' by a roundabout way hauling the 15 50 Old Docks-Llandilo Jct. special banana train. (See photo in the first instalment of this series - Page 32 of Issue 6 of 'SW'.) Help came towards the end of 1960, when some 9Fs (I think the total was five) were transferred to Eastleigh so giving the SR much more control of motive power hauling these heavy trains.

Staunch steam aficionados were doubtless aghast at the coming of the Cl. 33 type and the February 1963 WTT supplement first denoted which trains would become DL hauled. It has to be said that their coming negated the requirement for double-heading on the branch, although this had already been reduced by the use of H16 and W class tanks, plus the need to change locomotives to a large tender engine. To increase line capacity on the branch, Marchwood loop was lengthened about 1960. To reduce the long section between there and Fawley, a completely new signal box and crossing loop of sufficient length to cross maximum length block trains, was opened in October 1960 at Frost Lane between Hythe and Fawley. It was destined, however, to have a relatively short life, as the loop was taken out of use and block post abolished in November 1980. The box lingered on until March 1981 when it finally closed upon conversion of the level crossing to AHBs.

On the same branch, mention should be made of Marchwood military sidings which provided a steady flow of military freight traffic and special troop trains. I recall it being particularly busy during the 1956 Suez crisis. On the passenger side, a new halt at Hardley, between Hythe and Fawley, was opened on 3 May 1958 to serve a nearby rubber product factory. It never appeared in public timetables, stops being unadvertised, and closed on 5 April 1965. The meagre passenger services saw modernisation in the shape of Hampshire DEMUs, at first con-

Left - Dieselisation comes to Hampshire. 2-car DEMU No. 1104 between Sholing and Netley on the Sunday 14.03 Southampton Central to Portsmouth. 14.20, 15 June 1958.

Opposite page - Due to restricted luggage space available on the DEMU sets, it was found necessary to introduce special parcels workings over certain of the routes traversed by the DEMU workings. One of these was between Salisbury and Portsmouth, resulting in T9 No. 30707 in charge of the 10.57 Salisbury to Portsmouth and Southsea photographed between Sholing and Netley at 13.20, 24 June 1960.

fined to the Sunday trips from 16 November 1958, taking over further trains in the summer 1962 timetable and all remaining services from that year's winter timetable. Also during that winter, Saturday and Sunday services were withdrawn. Complete withdrawal of passenger workings came on 14 February 1966.

Train Numbers

I suppose it can be said that compared with other regions, the SR did not have much to do with individual trains carrying identification numbers. London suburban EMUs carried letter headcodes - some inverted! - indicating line of route (- the famous 'HOVIS' on these trains) until this was replaced entirely by numeric headcodes (main line stock always carried a number code) with the coming of EPB stock in the early 1950s. This new system was continued when the DEMUs came along. By not conforming to lamp positioning on the front of engines to indicate class of train, the position of white discs (lamps at night) on SR steam locomotive fronts indicated the line of route. Nevertheless, at busy times such as summer Saturdays with a procession of trains all heading, say towards Bournemouth and all carrying the same disc headcode, the code did not give away details as to any out of course running. Thus on summer Saturdays, from about the 1950s onwards, train numbers were carried by trains to and from Waterloo, and on summer Sundays, by trains to Waterloo arriving there after approximately 17.00. Individual numbers were carried on headboards affixed by Operating staff in the centre of the smokebox beneath the locomotive chimney. The WTT instructed that if this was not done, the TSO had to be advised. I do not remember seeing any instructions as to what to do in the

case of a station advising us that this had not been done, but suppose the TSO would have advised signalboxes. Numbers were 4XX and 2XX in down and up directions respectively but up Channel Islands boat trains from Southampton Old Docks seemed to be exempt from this practice! Up Weymouth and Bournemouth trains had these boards affixed at Bournemouth Central but some, such as Lymington Pier-Waterloo trains, had them fixed at Southampton Central.

Cross-country services on the Portsmouth-Bristol-Cardiff axis, carried boards from the starting station but on the handful of through trains from Brighton, they were fixed at Fareham. Bournemouth Central was delegated to fix headboards to the 08.48 New Milton - Swansea and 09.00 Bournemouth Central –Cardiff, both via Fordingbridge. As SR locomotives on these trains did not work through to the WR or vice versa, Salisbury had to fix boards on trains to Portsmouth. These trains carried individual numbers, until the adoption in the 1950s, of a letter indicating the region of destination. Thus trains to the WR were numbered 1VXX and to the SR 1OXX. Through trains via Basingstoke and Oxford also carried this style of headcode.

Hampshire Diesels

Until 16 September 1957 local travel in south Hampshire could be a very sedate affair, often with lengthy gaps (particularly on Sundays) between trains. On Sundays for instance, in the 1957 summer timetable, the first arrival at Portsmouth & Southsea from Southampton was not until 11.14. Conversely and in fairness, however, it has to be said that in steam days peak period frequency at Netley line stations was far better

than today's electric service. Although by the time the DEMUs arrived, many Drummond 4-4-0s had been replaced by Std. Cl. 4 2-6-0s, rolling stock was a mixture of corridor and ex-L&SWR 3-LAV non-corridor sets. In addition, several inter-regional services between Cardiff / Bristol and Portsmouth became local services between Salisbury and Portsmouth. All this changed upon arrival of the diesels, with far increased frequencies as under:

Hourly (weekdays & Sundays) Portsmouth & Southsea - Salisbury via Southampton Central semi-fast. Hourly (weekdays & Sundays) Portsmouth & Southsea - Southampton Central stopping extended to Andover Jct. from summer1962, so providing two trains hourly between Portsmouth and Southampton.
Hourly (weekdays & Sundays) Portsmouth & Southsea - Andover Jct. via Eastleigh stopping although some Sunday trains were truncated at Romsey where the whole of this service terminated from summer 1962.
Hourly (weekdays) Southampton Terminus -Winchester City.
Hourly (weekdays & Sundays) Southampton Terminus (weekdays) / Southampton Central (Sundays) -Alton, so giving a weekday frequency of two trains per hour between Southampton Terminus and Winchester City.

Sunday reductions were introduced in the winter 1958 timetable when some stations lost their Sunday service in winter whilst others had theirs reduced. The CTC wanted us TSO staff to receive our new WTTs as soon as possible to enable us to study and familiarise ourselves with the new service. Unfortunately late rolling stock delivery (nothing ever changes) meant the complete timetable was postponed until 4 November 1957. In the interim period, the Mid-Hants line had to make do with the existing steam P&P service of nine weekday and four

Sunday trains, whereas when the diesels finally arrived, there were sixteen weekday and fifteen Sunday trains. Rolling stock late arrival meant that the full regular interval service did not operate from day one, as Portsmouth & Southsea - Andover Jct. and some peak period Netley line 'extras' were steam-hauled until 4 November (at slower timings than the DEMUs, of course).

Originally the diesels were built as 2-car units, most trains being formed of a single unit. This inevitably caused overcrowding problems at times, especially during peak periods and when bank holiday weekends coincided with fine weather. Here the TSO stepped in as it was often possible to stop inter-regional trains, which by that time called only at principal stations between Salisbury and Portsmouth, at stations where passengers had been left behind by arranging for 'special stop' orders to be issued to train crews, a typical note explaining this problem on Easter Monday 1958 was reproduced on p.143 of the May 1958 'RO': *"On the Portsmouth to Salisbury service, the diesel cars could not accommodate all passengers; most were overcrowded and passengers were even left behind, in spite of poor weather. Two steam reliefs were run between Portsmouth and Southampton, (6.10 pm Portsmouth to Southampton Central, and 7.16 p.m. Portsmouth to Southampton Terminus) worked by U No. 31806 and T9 No. 30707. A new innovation was the extension of the 4.35 p.m. Exeter Central through to Portsmouth and Southampton."* (The two relief services were clearly pre-arranged as they appear in the Special Traffic notice and were not TSO arranged.) Additional steam-hauled services were soon arranged by the Special Traffic section at times of anticipated heavy traffic and during the peak summer school holiday season. Some relief from this situation came when an additional third car was built for all units from the summer of 1959. By December 1959 nearly all the units had become three cars. In addition, four further units (Nos. 1123-1126) were constructed, which effectively put an end to steam reliefs from January 1960.

Recognition should be made of the public timetable compilers at Waterloo, as all dated service ramifications were included in the Winter 1957 and subsequent timetables. From the summer 1962 timetable the Southampton Terminus - Winchester City was extended to Reading General, also running on Sundays. Prior to this service being extended to Reading, on summer Saturdays from 1958 to 1961 inclusive, many Southampton Terminus - Winchester City trains were diverted to the DN&SR Winchester Chesil station to relieve congestion at Winchester City that would have undoubtedly arisen during terminating and starting manoeuvres. To cater for running to Reading, seven further units (Nos. 1127-1133) were built which had larger brake vans than the original units. This extra brake van space was provided by losing one bay of seating; these units were distinguishable by an additional brake van window.

As originally built the DEMUs were noisy: no silencers were fitted; they were rough riding, had poor heating and interior draughts. Gradually modifications were undertaken to eliminate these problems - unit 1117 being the first fitted with a silencer and noted as such on 15 November 1957.
Once the interior heating difficulties had been resolved, they became comfortably warm, a feature much appreciated during the bitter 1962/63 winter. Once all problems had been resolved, the Hampshire DEMUs gave a generally reliable service.

When unit failures did occur, if at all possible the following DEMU train was sent to assist the stricken unit; however this was not always successful. For instance, the first major failure came about on 21 September 1957. The following Salisbury-Portsmouth & Southsea was despatched from Woolston to push the recalcitrant unit, but when coupled, both units were unable to move. Fortunately the train behind the Salisbury one was the steam-hauled 07.13 Southampton Terminus - Fareham parcels which in turn became the rescuer. Reference must also be made to the problems with these diesel units on the Mid-Hants line. Two car units seemed fine but when they became three cars the steep gradients 'over the Alps' seemed more taxing. At the time a rumour abounded that in winter periods, to provide some extra power, some drivers switched-off the carriage heating when going uphill. I don't know whether there was any substance in this rumour. Further problems occurred in wet autumn periods with wheel slip on the line on the three car trains. I recall a traction inspector travelled on the 13.50 Southampton Terminus - Alton on 13 November 1959 and so much time was lost (the weather being rain accompanied by a south westerly gale) that by the time Alton was reached, a decision was made to detach the centre coach and return with two cars. I think this was the first occasion 'leaves on the line' caused headaches, an autumn condition which continues to plague railway operation. By the next day Alton trains were reduced to two cars, but a third car was restored from 5 December 1959. Subsequently two car units Nos. 1121/2 were transferred from the South Eastern Division for Alton line services and remained in service for many years. Another problem on this line was with timekeeping due to quick turnarounds at either end. To illustrate this difficulty, on Sundays there was only four and six minutes turnaround at Alton and Southampton Central respectively. The TSO watched especially for the timekeeping of these trains and quite often the diesels, with their superior acceleration, were given preference over late running steam hauled trains. To aid timekeeping the Shawford stop was omitted by most weekday, and all Sunday trains, from the winter 1960 and winter 1961 timetables respectively.

Left - *No. 34009 'Lyme Regis' passing Broadstone with the diverted 12.30 down, the Bournemouth Belle working, 15.20, Sunday 3 April 1960.*

Top right - *No. 34085 '501 Squadron' between Lyndhurst Road and Beaulieu Road with the 15.12 Westbury to Poole freight. The working appears to be comprised almost entirely of Presflo cement wagons. 18.05, 31 July 1965.*

Bottom right - *Two 'U' class engines, Nos. 31623 and 31626 passing St. Denys at 11.10 with the special 11.03 Southampton Terminus - Eastleigh ECS working. 8 July 1961.*

Photographs by Richard Simmons

TO BE CONTINUED

Top - One of the earliest views of Brighton Works, circa 1870. Subsequent redevelopment in 1908/10, meant most of that seen was swept away with the exception of the office block - located beneath the windmill. The line to Lewes and its associated viaduct is visible surrounded by what was then open countryside.
Bottom - An interesting comparison recorded in 1940 and before much damage was done by bombing to the west side wall.

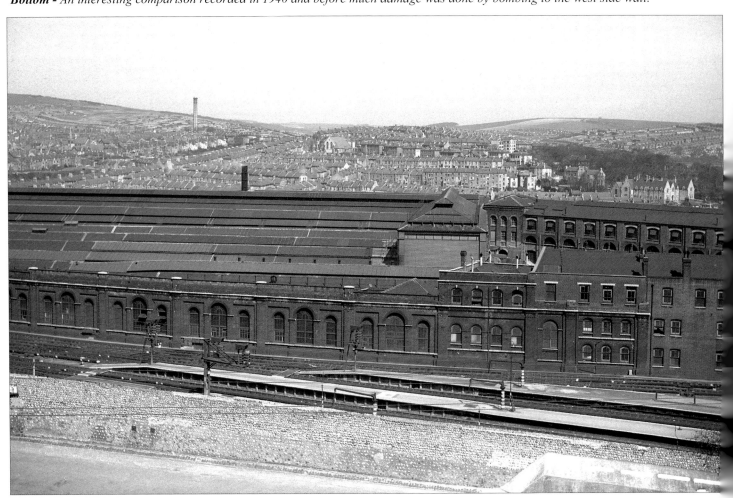

BRIGHTON WORKS MEMORIES

More stories from his apprentice days by Brian Potts

There are a good number of excellent books about the 'Brighton', including those with illustrations from the nineteenth century. From these it is possible to see that the loco works, which latterly occupied the complete site, had in those early days, also been the location of the engine shed, the latter subsequently removed to its well-known position, in the 'V' of the lines to London and Hove, in 1861.

In 'Rail Centres Brighton' (Ian Allan), page 56, there is a photograph from the west dated circa 1870. Latterly the only buildings from this view which remained intact were the Office Block (under the windmill), at just 35' long and that to the right hand side which was the Wheel Shop, 190' long – later to be the Carpenter's Shop etc. The roof of this was later raised and a further storey added. This new top floor formed the canteen reached by wooden open stairs in two rises.

With redevelopment of the works site, the Wheel Shop became part of the west bay, at the south end of the Erecting Shop. The Office Block later had on the top floor the SR No. 2 Drawing Office. On the ground floor of this block was a passageway, off which were the Doctor's and Ambulance room and also other offices. This passage led all the way from the south end to New England Street, via the bridge over the goods line, passed the Pay Office and then down concrete steps, in three stages, to street level. This passage was 100' long but only 10' wide, which when filled up at home times with workers emptying from the various shops, could became very congested. The bridge over the goods lines was wider, at some 25'. Another exit was through the old Brass Foundry and to Trafalgar Street and the station, via a set of steps upwards, now no longer extant. Office staff also had access direct to the platform. There were a number of buildings which ran across the south yard: these were all removed on the works rebuild of 1908/10.

The tallest of the new buildings provided around this time, was a completely new four-sided construction and housed the Boiler Shop 'Iron Man' – a hydraulic riveter, boilers being lifted up vertically from the firebox end with the drum placed over the rivet doll.

In the past this structure has been incorrectly referred to as the new Erecting Shops, which of course ran north to south, rather than west to east as did the Iron Man building. The latter was also nowhere near as tall as the former. The Erecting Shop gained its height from new steelwork between the west and east bays, commensurate with which the outer walls were raised and the building re-roofed and new interior travelling cranes added (1908) on higher tracking. The original steel work was of round contour, the new being fabricated of 'I' section and plates. Originally, the north end of the east bay - where it abutted the machine shop had been open, but was later blocked in, apart from a passage way through.

All the shops had woodblock floors, intended to avoid damage to parts if they fell. Work benches and the standing position of the various machine operators had duckboards raised slightly higher than floor level. In this way any swarf or other items would pass through. On a Friday afternoon, the last hour of work was spent lifting these boards, cleaning underneath and also cleaning the beds and sides of the lathes and machines. They were also oiled as necessary. Waste metal, turnings etc, was segregated into the appropriate bins, either brass or steel.

The shop employees had a works number and collected a small square brass plate with this identification stamped on it from the Timekeeper's desk. This was both in the morning and afternoon. If late, you were docked time in ¼ hour segments. In addition when you did eventually arrive at your allotted workspace this was accompanied by colleagues hammering on their own benches and cheering.

This desk, where we collected our plates from, was sited near the stairs leading to the Timekeeper's office, which was above the drawing store, at the south end of the machine shop. On leaving work, these brass plates were thrown into collecting bins. (At other times and indeed at other works, the terms '(pay) checks', 'discs' or 'tickets' have been used to identify what in my time were referred to as 'plates'.)

The Machine Shop itself contained, as the name implies, all types of machinery, ordinary centre lathes, turret lathes which had positions for six tools which could be used one at a time, planing, lapping and boring machines. In addition there were shaping machines and radial drills, most of the equipment being new in 1942 and independently motor-driven. Old photographs showed

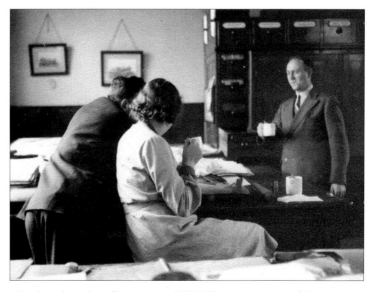

Tea break in the offices, circa 1938. Those present are left: Alastair Lawson, sitting Mary ? - later his wife, and right: Frank Knight. Both the men were still there when I was an apprentice. I recall Frank giving me a scale rule, 6" long: he was due to retire shortly afterwards. Howard Butler collection

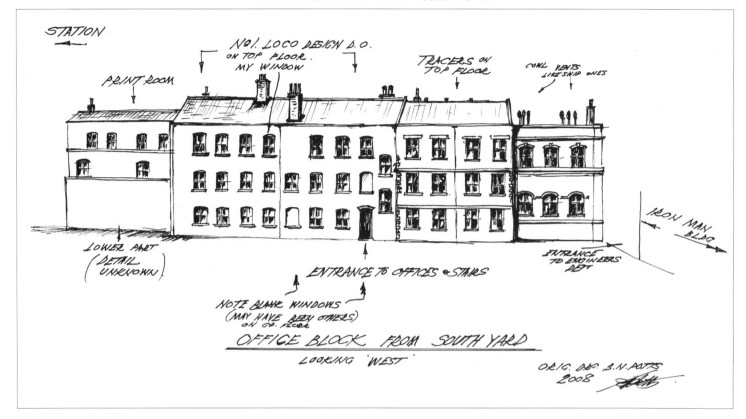

OFFICE BLOCK FROM SOUTH YARD
LOOKING 'WEST'

that earlier machines had been belt-driven from overhead shafts, as indeed was the norm in engineering premises for many years. The largest machine was called a 'Stirk Hiloplane' on which cylinders etc. would have the frame bolting faces planed.

A flame-cutting machine was sited at the north end of the Machine Shop using oxy-acetylene gas, and used for cutting out items of plating, flanges etc. There was a large marking-out table between the Machine and Fitting Shops.

Some of the men had a habit of singing whilst at work. One I recall doing this was Dave Garnet, who would burst into a rendition of 'Behind the Green Door' – the song made famous by Frankie Vaughan: most of apprentices in the Fitting Shop would also join in the chorus. Don Pleasance would also sing some ditties: one I recall as 'Don't go down to the mine Daddy – you may not come home tonight.'

In the Coppersmiths', new pipes would be made from copper. Steel rod, bent to the correct curves and offsets and to the correct lengths on the centre line, would be used as jigs. Flanges were then either brazed on or soldered, the finished product often emerging in the salmon colour of soft copper. When all the pipes required for an engine under repair were returned to the erecting shop and placed on the ground, it often looked a right old jumble with so many different shapes and lengths. Some perhaps were obvious in their use, but others, particularly the various small section lubrication pipes needed some sorting out, especially if they had become bent en-route.

Entering the east bay of the Erecting Shop from the south, there was soon on the right hand side an entrance from the Smiths' and Light Plating shops. After this, and about one-third of the length down the shop, was an opening to the left with a track running out. This led from the Boiler Shop, through its wall

and doors across the west bay and across to the east bay: just prior to this was one of the old air raid shelters and a large air receiver. At about two-thirds of the length of the shops on the right hand side, was the entrance from the Machine and Fitting Shops, located between the Drawing Store and Main Stores.

Both the east and west bays had three roads each, with only the centre ones being connected at either end, via sliding doors to the outside world. Pits ran on the outer roads for a small part of the north end of the east bay centre road, which was where locomotive wheeling took place. There were no pits at the south end of the west bay, from the boiler shop entrance. The reason for this was this was the Wheel Shop with its large wheel-turning lathes on the west wall. Pits were unnecessary for this line of work, as well as potential hazard.

Within the Erecting Shop, each allocated engine space had white lines painted around the outside around which no items or parts were to be placed. This ensured access and transport routes were kept clear.

There were a number of overhead cranes in the works. There were three in the west bay, of 25 tons, 35 tons and 40 tons. The east bay had two, both of 35 tons and from Cravens of Manchester. These were dated as being installed in 1908. The Boiler Shop and its two bays had different capacity cranes. The west bay had one 20 ton and one 30 ton crane. The east had two slightly smaller cranes, of 12 tons each. The Iron Man building went across the south end of both bays with its own 30 ton crane.

Lifting of locos was done by two cranes, each double hook mounted. Special double wire strops with double shackles at each end were used, with the hook below and around the buffer beam and inside of the buffers, and similarly at the dragbox end. Some engines had holes for this purpose provided in

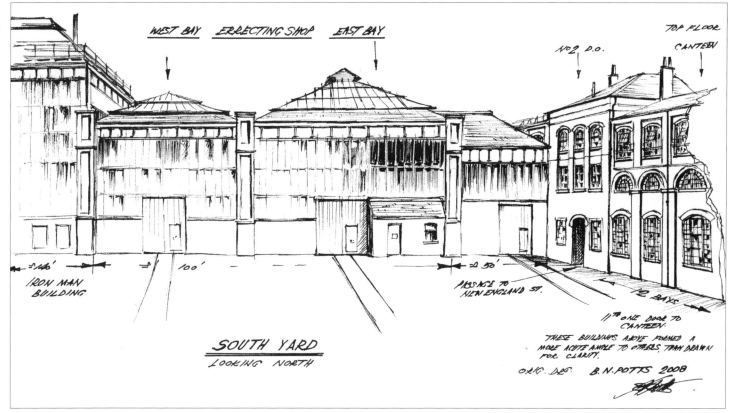

WEST BAY ERRECTING SHOP EAST BAY

TOP FLOOR
CANTEEN

NO 2 D.O.

IRON MAN
BUILDING

≈146'   100'

≈ 50'

PASSAGE TO
NEW ENGLAND ST.

12 BAYS

11TH ONE DOOR TO
CANTEEN

THESE BUILDINGS ABOVE FORMED A
MORE ACUTE ANGLE TO OTHERS, THAN DRAWN
FOR CLARITY.

ORIG. DWG.   B. N. POTTS 2008

SOUTH YARD
LOOKING NORTH

the frames in the cab area, e.g. the BR 2-6-4T. In this case the aft crane strop came in through the cab roof shutters. Otherwise cab roofs usually had a removable section, so the lift could go vertically to the drag beam. The actual lifting operations was directed by a man known as the 'Slinger' who would use various hand movements to direct the crane drivers high above.

Boilers – smaller ones were lifted with a single large chain around the drum, near to the firebox end and on the centre of gravity. Larger ones required two cranes, in which case a single chain was placed around the drum near the smokebox end and the other at the firebox end with a chain put inside the firebox and around a large block of wood. To move boilers through the wall opening and doors of the boiler shop, a trolley was used. This had four wheels about one foot in diameter mounted on a bogie type arrangement and ran on a cross track. The boiler barrel and firebox would hang well over this trolley at both ends as it was pinch barred along: it always looked extremely precarious. In my time at Brighton, I never saw a W/C or B/B have its boiler off as 'Generals' were done at Eastleigh on these classes. However as numbers of the type were built at Brighton, the boilers must have arrived and been lifted on to the frames of the new engines.

Transport of parts not needing a crane, might be by chainblocks - near benches and machines, or by sack barrow, bigger trolleys and also electrically driven trolleys . There were trays about 4' x 5' with lifting lugs on the corners on which engine parts were placed, the crane would lift these if the engine changed its location in the shops.

One of the most daunting experiences for a young apprentice was that of wheeling an engine. Despite its weight, the whole process of lifting an engine and then putting it down correctly on to its wheels and axle boxes was a delicate operation.

Firstly, the wheels were put into the correct position, or as near as could be, and the engine then lifted above. Men were stationed in the pit: one at each axlebox, and whose purpose was to guide the axleboxes into the horns as they lowered. One's first experience of this was memorable as a locomotive was seemingly lowered down on you. Additionally, men were spaced around outside, each to shout 'stop' if necessary. Lowering was again under the control of the slinger. When complete, horn wedges were then put on and secured. The actual springs are recalled as heavy and awkward to manoeuvre into place with a nasty habit of toppling over on to the pit board or worse, down the pit – mind your feet!

After wheeling it was time to add the coupling rods. These were first placed on the floor when required. They were then assembled and lined up shoulder to shoulder. Manpower was used to lift them off the floor and on to the crank pins, these and the connecting rods understandably being pretty heavy things. Eventually all were secured with collar nuts, gudgeon pins and more nuts.

I recall a couple of golden rules told when starting in the works, obvious perhaps, but important enough to repeat. Firstly not to put fingers into holes in an attempt to line up pins etc, and equally important not to tread on running rails or points. One of the fitters in the works had a wooden leg due to a point closing and trapping his foot - a loco then ran over it. Southern men were also told to step over rails as a matter of habit because of some rails being electrified.

Whilst in the training school, I recall one lunch time seeing one of the newly built BR 2-6-4Ts being got ready for her trial run, and asking Bill Long, the trials driver, if I could go aboard. He was quiet for a moment and then seemed to mellow asking if I really did want to come along. I was advised to ask Reg Nunn, who was in charge of the apprentices. Unfortunately

Left - *The roof of the works on fire probably following the enemy raid of 18 May 1942.*

Opposite - *Seen from the offices looking down on to the east side of the station. The extremity of Platform 9 is just visible on the extreme left with the coaches in Platform 8. In Platform 7 is a 6PUL unit with Pullman Car 'Iris': possibly meaning this was unit No. 2016 / 3016. The Marsh 4-4-2T in the dock may well be performing station pilot duties.*

Howard Butler collection, circa 1938.

my request was denied, for the simple reason I was still in the training school. I was naturally extremely disappointed, although later, when in the Erecting Shop, there were lots of similar opportunities which I was glad to take.

Moving on to this time, locomotives destined for trial - new or after repair - were prepared outside the north end of the works and near the big green 'Brighton' sign with its arrow underneath. Attached was a device consisting of a pipe with a ring with holes in, similar to a blower and connected to an air line. This was placed down the chimney and had the same effect of drawing the smoke and fumes through the tubes not only to reduce the time spend in raising steam but also to reduce the sulphurous fumes that would otherwise make life very unpleasant for the men still working in the cab and roundabout. This was the time the final jobs, like 'Chippy' putting in the cab floorboards, tightening up fittings, pulling up mud-hole door nuts, were undertaken. When in steam, no matter how tight the latter had been made before, you could guarantee they would need doing again!

When the engine was ready for the off, the shunt signal would come off and with drain cocks belting out steam we were soon on to the viaduct, the height of which was much more apparent from the footplate than from a coach seat. Trials invariably went east towards Lewes, sometimes Uckfield or Groombridge, the quieter routes being used so that in the event of a breakdown less delay would ensue to other traffic.

To a youthful apprentice, the variation in height of fireholes above the cab floor was noticeable, some being really uncomfortable to fire, like a 'T9' or 'M7' which had the bottom of the firehole only about nine inches above the floor, compared with a 'WC/BB' at 15 inches, or a 'Schools' at twenty inches. Then of course there were the different type of doors themselves.

The 'Schools' were real powerhouses, quite superb, although why the first 10 had such uncomfortably low side windows and cut outs I don't know. The noise made was also different on various classes and certainly different to that heard as a passenger in a coach, more of a rumbling. The blast was also

heard through the firebox and its pull on the fire affected the brightness in the cab, people's faces and the edges of the folds in clothing were highlighted, an eerie but magic quality came over the whole scene. Initially it came as quite a surprise to me how much engines and tenders swayed at speed – invariably in opposite directions as well. Consequently it was a matter of getting your 'sea legs', or more appropriately 'footplate legs'. I always enjoyed my trips.

In 1956 a fellow Brighton apprentice who lived at Redhill and knew a number of the crews from that shed, asked me if I would like to go with him on a passenger turn with one of the new 'Class 4' 2-6-0s coupled to a high sided tender. The trip was arranged, Redhill – Reading – Redhill, the engine No. 76056. We joined the footplate at Redhill, the booked fireman saying little other than 'You won't need me', and disappeared back into the train, travelled to Reading and back on the cushions. We left about 6.00 pm and returned just before midnight including going on to the Southern shed at Reading.

It was a new experience to be on the footplate in the dark. The fire was also pretty clinkered up, so to get a fire-iron from the tunnel in the tender, it needed to be manoeuvred outside some way. The driver told us when it was clear and safe to do. We also rocked the fire-grate on shed and turned the engine. Consequently with a cleaner fire bed, we had a better trip back, indeed it was quite a lively run. Whilst at Reading we also enjoyed a pint in the pub opposite Tudor Road, near what was then the Eames model shop – now long gone.

Back at Brighton I was now employed in the Erecting Shop where, if working under an engine you might be reaching up from the pit, or on a pit board - which had five planks with two stretcher battens. These were placed across a pit and were moveable to other positions. One day I was lying on one of these with my legs out and working at something above me. When I tried to get up I could not, my feet were stuck. I then discovered my boots had been welded by their steel toe caps to the engine frames – I had to remove my boots and chip them off.

During WW2 the works at Brighton suffered considerable bomb damage, the entire wall of the shops next to the Lewes running line destroyed and subsequently replaced from here around to the Office Block with three drops of corrugated sheeting above new brick posts and windows, there being only one part from one of the original sections left. Originally these sections had three concealed windows, the centre being larger but destroyed in an air raid. There is a view of this damage to the roof with fires being put out on Page 21 of 'Brighton Behind the Front'.

In my first article in 'SW' (Issue No.1), I mentioned that valve liners sometimes needed to be cut out with a chisel. One such time was on a 'W/C'. I recall I did the back liner with a fitter doing the other. Charlie Stuvold, the charge hand of the valve setting gang, came to see how we were doing, my progress being considerably more than the other chap. Charlie could not believe his eyes when he saw he had not cut up to and beyond the port but had cut through the port bar, in other words the whole length without the advantage of the port openings.

One of the characters in the lifting shops was called David, a giant of a chap at 6' 8", he did all the brake gear and was always covered in rust looking like how Red Indians were then portrayed on film. Parts such as these, when taken off engines, had numbers stamped on to alloy plates which were wired up to them, before the whole was put in the 'bosh', a caustic soda bath, sited outside the north end of the works, between the east

and west shops. It was in the same house as the air compressors, but I never went inside here. I recall one of the labourers, a certain 'Horace', had an accident with the bosh, resulting in his admission to the burns unit at East Grinstead hospital.

Often in pictures of locomotives in works, can be seen the letter 'F' chalked or scribed on the front of the chimney plus the loco number, The reason being that when an engine is first built, a lot of trouble is spent in lining up the centre of the chimney to the centre of the blastpipe, using a device which is set up vertically. With the chimney then aligned, securing holes are then drilled through the smokebox. If this was not done the result would be poor steaming.

Sadly work on locomotives no longer takes place at Brighton today: indeed the works were demolished some ago. Instead the site has been totally redeveloped with apartments, a hotel, shops, supermarket and car park, the latter approximately where the offices once were, abutting the Lewes line.

Little tangible is thus left, although the columns which once supported the fitting shops etc, are still visible from New England Road.. I do wonder how many, if any, of the residents know what was there beforehand and the great history of the works. Perhaps the street names might be the only clue, Stroudley, Billinton – that is to someone with an enquiring mind.

Finally with thanks to the friend, of Dave from Emsworth, who reminded me his surname, of course, Garnet. I was sorry to hear he is no longer with us.

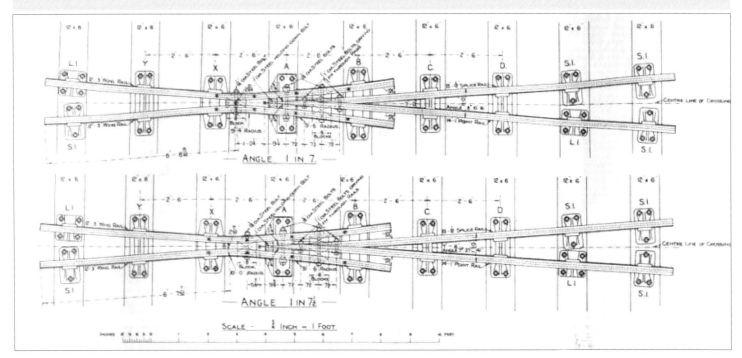

Crossings

Extract from a drawing of 1:7 and a 1:7 ½ common crossing.

The Southern Railway standards for new build switch and crossing (S&C) initially laid out in 1924, which were the result of adopting details developed for most railway companies by the REA, contain many detailed drawings. To illustrate the detail available to the designer, the manufacturer of new track and 'the end user', I have used detail from two larger drawings in the standard collection of drawings printed in 1926.

The first drawing is for the common crossings for a 1:7 and a 1:7½ angle crossing. It shows the level of detail laid out for the designer to adopt and shows how the two rails of the vee of the crossing were matched and connected by bolts and blocks. The point rail is the longer of the two rails which form the vee of the crossing, on the right in this drawing, and it extends to the nose (the sharp point) of the crossing. This should be the rail in the route carrying the greatest traffic. Normally this is the straight or through line, but sometimes if the traffic was significantly heavier on the turnout, the point rail in the crossing might favour this line. The other rail forming the vee of the crossing is the splice rail and, as its name suggests, is spliced into the side of the point rail. It does not extend to the nose. The two rails in front of the vee of the crossing are the wing rails. These are shown to the left in the drawing. They effectively form check rails to either side of the crossing, particularly guiding wheels through the area immediately around the nose where the wheel weight is transferred from the wing rail to the point or splice rail

when travelling from left to right. They are also, of course, extended past the nose of the crossing to provide the vital strength and rigidity at this area which sees considerable 'pounding' by passing wheels. The chair positions for the crossing are shown. Chair A is a 'slab and bracket' chair with a through bolt to hold the components together. This chair is always the A chair and the chairs supporting the vee progress through B, C, D etc. and will be followed by the crossing angle, in the identification of the chair, so D7 /D 7 ½ etc. The physical spread between the two rails forming the crossing vee will vary, according to the crossing angle, as the timber spacing normally remains around 2'6". The chairs in front of the vee holding the wing rail fronts are X, Y etc.

Extract from a drawing of the first stretcher bar for straight-cut switches.

This second extract from the standards again shows a small part of the detail drawn to illustrate how straight-cut switches are attached to the first stretcher bar. This is the bar which holds the two moveable switch rails at the set distance apart near the toe of the switch. There are normally at least two stretcher bars to all switches, some longer switches have several. The main difference on the first bar is that it is extended at each end for attaching to the rod system, which drives the points and is seen as the flat end portion with bolt hole. The other important point of this stretcher bar is that it extends closely under the two outside stock rails irrespective of which side the switch rail is actually open. This prevents any tendency for the switch to be lifted upwards in relation to the stock rail and possibly cause a wheel flange to strike and part the closed switch and stock, which

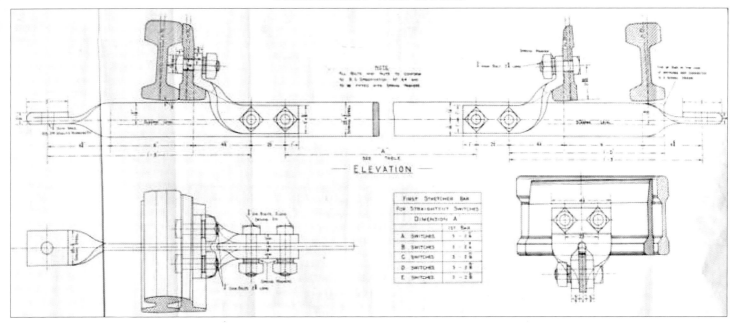

would lead to a derailment. Typically this happens on short switches where the wheel leaves the other end of the switch near the heel and presses down here, tending to lift the switch toe upwards. For this reason this extension, which is not repeated on the following stretcher bars is sometimes referred to as the 'kicking strap or bar'.

Photo 7 (right) Spring Crossing Sandown IOW.

This is a spring crossing still in everyday active service, albeit it is on the Isle of Wight!

The Southern used these crossings extensively on routes where the diverging line was rarely used and of slow speed. As there is no gap in support for the wheel in the crossing area (in the crossing's normal position) there is less impact on the crossing. The curved moveable wing rail lies immediately against the crossing nose. For normal use in the through route the wheel passes through the right hand 'normal' side of the crossing and the flange gap between the straight wing rail and crossing vee. When a wheel passes through the turnout line on the left, the flange pushes the closed wing rail over in the slide chairs and compresses the spring in the round container. The wheel is pulled over to the correct side of the crossing by the adjacent turnout check rail, to avoid the flange striking the crossing nose, so the track gauge is very critical in this area. After the wheel flange passes clear of the crossing it simply springs back by the action of the compressed and contained spring. Approaching from the 'leg' (lower end in photograph) end of the crossing, the curved extended end of the wing rail catches the flange and pulls the rail over. Spring crossings were only ever used at slow speeds as their action in use is quite 'clunky', but they were surprisingly common on the Southern Railway. This is the last known survivor in common use.

This is a recent photograph, but note the IOW track (Network Rail) is still largely ballasted with shingle, once very common through many areas of the Southern railway system. Re-ballasting now uses granite which is imported to the Island, but it will take many years to change all the ballast. This shingle

ballast has very little ability to 'lock' together like angular granite, so it is far less suitable to retain modern high speed, high axle-loading lines but there is no suitable quarry on the IOW and importing stone is expensive.

Fishplates

Photo 8 (below) This is of an Ellson Old Type fishplate joint from 1942.

This was developed to try to give better support at the fishplated joint by forming continuous support, very much like the modern adjustment switch. A large cast slab spanned two sleepers and a large bracket extended to the rail head on the outside face of the rails, thus providing wheel support over the actual rail joint. A more normal two bolt fishplate was used on the inside of the rail. Theoretically all the rail surfaces in this joint wore equally. This was trialled but not adopted. It is believed this was also trialled in America.

This form of joint would be classified as a type of fully supported joint, whereas the normal joints are suspended type, hanging between chairs. Other trials in the early days of railways used a single chair to support both rail ends. This was not very successful on lines as speeds and weights increased, but on lightly-laid earlier lines, particularly very early horse-drawn lines, which still existed feeding the bigger railway, it sometimes remained.

More common was the use of two bolt fishplates and some low speed lines and sidings still have these. When this system was used it was important to place the joint sleepers much closer together, so the chairs were effectively either end of the fishplate to give it maximum support and stop the tendency for the shorter fishplate to work loose.

Photo 9 (Opposite column)

Junction Fishplates between a BH rail on the left and Flat Bottom on the right are shown in the photograph, which also contains the detail on the fishplate side of where to use them. The fishplate in front of the joint shows a crack from bottom towards the top which can be a particular weakness in this style of stepped fishplate. Extra metal 'ribs' are now used on the outside of these forged fishplates. All inspections of the track pay particular care to the state of fishplates.

The area which references the two rails together is at the top. The rails must match perfectly on their head with no step, but equally the fishplate must fit the web space between the rail head and the foot snugly and avoid any movement due to a gap. Fishplates are bevelled top and bottom to fit into correspondingly bevelled surfaces of the underside of the head and top of the foot of the rail. The action of tightening the fishbolts pulls the plates tighter into this coned area. They are not actually normally in contact with the rail web.

Fishplates which are 'straight' will be used to match two similar rails which are new or have equal wear. If the rails are worn to different degrees, then fishplates are available in 1/16 in. steps, to compensate for normal wear of the rail head, up to ¼ in. Add to this the matching of similar or dissimilar rail sections such as BH 85lb or 95lb, FB sections such as 98lb, 109lb, 113lb or the more modern 113A rail (different rail height to 113 lb/yd rail) and the number of fishplates increases. Even more variety was found as the pre group companies such as the LSWR had longer fishplates with different hole spacing. Then, of course, there were the insulated fishplates to separate rails for signalling electrical reasons. At this time these were made of a composite material - hardwood and resin in layers - and therefore weaker in strength than a metal fishplate.

The P.Way stores in the days of the Southern Railway could therefore contain a bewildering range of fishplates!

Issue No. 13 of *THE SOUTHERN WAY* (ISBN 978-1-906419-46-2) should be available in January 2011 at £12.95

Contents will (we hope) include BR Mk1 coaching stock on the Southern Region by Mike King,, a unique insight into the career of a former Ashford apprentice who rose to a senior position under Bulleid, an unusual perspective on the 'Schools' by Jeffery Grayer, more on 'Pull-Push' sets, LSWR 'demountables', the Fovant Military Railway - plus our usual features.

To receive your copy the moment it is released, order in advance from your usual supplier, or direct from the publisher:

Kevin Robertson (Noodle Books) PO Box 279, Corhampton, SOUTHAMPTON, SO32 3ZX

Tel 01489 877880

www.noodlebooks.co.uk